Costing and Pricing in the Digital Age

A practical guide
for information services

D0916508

Costing and Pricing in the Digital Age
A practical guide for information services

Herbert Snyder

Assistant Professor, School of Library and Information Science, Indiana University, USA

and

Elisabeth Davenport

Senior Lecturer and Subject Area Leader in Information Management, Department of Communication and Information Studies, Queen Margaret College, Edinburgh, UK

NEAL-SCHUMAN PUBLISHERS, INC.

NEW YORK

Published by
Neal-Schuman Publishers, Inc.
100 Varick Street
New York
NY 10013-1506

First published 1997

Library of Congress Cataloging-in-Publication Data

Snyder, Herbert.
        Costing and pricing in the digital age : a practical guide for
    information services / Herbert Snyder and Elisabeth Davenport.
            p.   cm.
        Includes bibliographical references and index.
        ISBN 1-55570-311-9
        1. Libraries--Special collections--Electronic information
    resources--Costs--Accounting. 2. Information services--Costs-
    -Accounting. 3. Electronic information resources--Costs-
    -Accounting.   I. Davenport, Elisabeth. II. Title.
    Z692.C65S69 1997
    025.1'1--dc21

Typeset from authors' disks in 11pt Century Old Style and
11pt Humanist by Library Association Publishing
Printed and made in Great Britain by Bookcraft (Bath) Ltd

Contents

Introduction

THE SCOPE OF THE TEXT

Information managers who work with networked services and systems may feel that technology has outpaced the development of accounting structures to regulate the resources under their control. Tangible information products can pose problems for cost-benefit analysis in any environment whether they are for profit or not for profit; intangible, distributed products and services present a bigger challenge. Library provision in the academic and public sector poses special problems, as it must often embrace a mixed economy which accommodates both a commitment to public good services on the part of users, and a cost-driven planning process on the part of public sector administrators.

Who should be responsible for network services which are spread across different cost centers? Who makes decisions on what should be purchased and how it is maintained? Can economic and fiscal models guide those who plan for electronic services? Should the costs of Internet be made more obvious with overt auditing of use and costs at every level, personal and institutional, or will this be seen as over-intrusive? What are the costs that are masked by site licensing and top-slicing? Can accounting practice be standardized? Such are the concerns of those who plan for information services in the digital world, at both macro and micro levels.

In 1992, a survey of computer services managers and librarians in the UK academic environment conducted by one of the authors showed a lack of consistency across institutions, with few using formal costing methods, or auditing usage. A later survey by the other author of public sector librarians in the US revealed similar gaps in practice.

There is a general need for more sophisticated accounting skills in all aspects of librarianship, as librarians are called upon to justify in financial terms the continuing provision of service in the face both of increased costs and decreased funding support. Many predict that migration to electronic services is a way to escape this negative feedback loop, as the digital path facilitates resource sharing, which should cut costs and improve customization, which in turn will contribute to service value. This assumption, though not unchallenged, lies behind our text. It is a primer for the practising librarian that will aid her or him to make financial judgments for the electronic provision of services. The text builds on standard principles of both managerial accounting and cost accounting, but is tailored to the provision of electronic services. We stress, however, that this is an introductory text. The interested reader is referred to more advanced treatments of the issues at various points in the chapters which follow.

Content

Chapter 1 ('Cost accounting and the library planning process: an introduction') introduces readers to the concepts and definitions of managerial and cost accounting. A brief explanation of accounting is provided as well as a rationale for the utility of these techniques to the practising librarian. We review practitioners' perceptions of problem areas. Examples are given of the use of financial data to assist managers in making decisions, and readers are introduced to standard methods of financial accounting and public reporting.

Chapter 2 ('Finding costs') covers cost concepts for managerial decision-making such as direct and indirect costs, allocated and overheads, fixed and variable costs, allocated and direct overheads, fixed and variable costs, discretionary, sunk and differential costs. These are discussed and illustrated in the context of standalone electronic equipment in libraries such as CD-ROM and photocopiers.

Chapter 3 ('Allocating costs') shows readers how to identify meaningful areas and activities in their organization where costs may be assigned: it shows you what you need to attach costs to. Once those activities have been identified the reader is introduced to techniques for collecting the financial data that will allow them to cost an activity such as running a server. This may involve a shift from looking at the purchase costs of owning or acquiring an asset to the activity costs of providing access: shifting the focal points of costing away from those previously considered important. Issues are discussed and examples provided, all in the context of electronic service provision.

Chapter 4 ('Threading your way through capital investment decisions') introduces financial decision-making techniques for library managers in an electronic environment. Using the techniques for financial data-gathering and the conceptual framework outlined in previous chapters, readers will be introduced to decision-making techniques tailored specifically to the electronic environment for providing electronic services: net present value, differential cost analysis and sensitivity analysis, in other words 'What's most likely to happen?', and 'How wrong can you afford to be?'.

Chapter 5 ('How much do we charge?') deals with questions of where costs are to be assigned and what systems to invest in and demonstrates that these are largely internal considerations. Using the cost and investment techniques presented in the previous chapters as a basis, the text takes the reader through the process of deciding how to price services. This chapter undertakes an explanation of costing strategies such as full-absorption versus marginal pricing; a more detailed analysis of allocating fixed and indirect costs; and an examination of cost-volume relationships through techniques such as break-even analysis.

Chapter 6 ('Conclusion') offers a review of the material covered in previous chapters, and places cost accounting techniques in a wider managerial context by showing how it may contribute to performance valuation and internal control.

The audience

We want our text to be of use to library professionals in the United Kingdom, the United States and indeed to anyone else needing a knowledge of standard costing and financial decision-making. It is likely to be of interest to at least three main groups:

1 Librarians and information managers in management and systems roles and other managers in networked environments (local or national government, for example) who work in a mixed public/private good economy, and who plan budgets which must accommodate network services.
2 Students/lecturers in librarianship and information management who may find that the text offers useful material for case-study work. The text is appropriate to different levels of course provision from national vocational qualifications and professional diploma to post-experience short courses.
3 Providers of electronic services or publishers who wish to work within the fiscal frameworks of their customers.

Structure

To make the text both readable and useful, we have organized the chapters into several sections. Each consists of a mix of scenarios (real-world narratives) and worked examples, which are linked to an analysis of a problem area and a discussion of techniques which will allow the manager to handle that problem. Most of the chapters also conclude with exercises. All of this material is based on the first-hand experience of the authors or of their students and colleagues; the financial data, though illustrative only, thus has some bearing on costs in the real world. A list of references is included at the end of relevant chapters as necessary.

Tell us about your experiences

We are happy to hear of readers' experiences in this area with a view to preparing further case studies. If you wish to contribute, contact the authors at:

hsnyder@indiana.edu

Please head your message "costs and prices".

Chapter 1

Cost accounting and the library planning process: an introduction

SHIFTING SANDS

There is increasing concern that the established foundations of fiscal practice are inadequate to support the complex of activities and tools that characterize public sector/not for profit librarianship in the 1990s. Budget constraints, the search for alternative funding, investment in technology and the development of complex vendor/customer relationships are only some of the problems facing library managers. If we are to trust the literature, it appears that 'libraries are being asked to perform what sounds like a magic trick. They are to downsize, economize, and streamline, while at the same time improve quality and provide customers with services they value, and, as if these challenges are not enough, libraries are in the midst of a fundamental transformation brought about by technology'.[1]

In many public sector institutions, the budget as opposed to profit and loss or revenue/expense statements remains the primary financial tool. But budgets are difficult to set in a distributed environment where institutional boundaries are blurred and users can choose from a range of service providers. Within the budget paradigm itself, there are difficulties. Current practice and the traditional division of budgets into operating, capital and personnel are increasingly difficult to sustain. In a recent study, two experienced practitioners suggest that the 'budget is only symbolic, since, in many cases certain kinds of expenditures are not included, and some, such as opportunity costs, cannot, because of their very nature, be included in a financial statement'.[2]

FISCAL FAQS

We have reviewed a number of texts which address the problems of budgeting for services provided in a shifting infrastructure and they indicate that a number of questions are commonly raised by practitioners faced with this predicament. Dunn and Martin, for example, provide a typical list of 'budgetary questions' associated with the 'new library':

- Are CD-ROM workstations capital equipment or the equivalent of periodical subscriptions?
- Have they replaced some elements of the traditional budget or added to them?
- How do you calculate the added utility costs of new electronic equipment and where should they appear on the budget?
- Are there other support costs that must be included in the budget?
- What are the different costs of space alternatives?
- What alternative uses could be made of any money saved on building construction?
- To what extent can mechanical and electronic systems replace staff costs, or will they simply be added budget items?[3]

We return to these and similar questions later in the text, offering advice on how to tackle the issues involved.

WHO NEEDS TO KNOW WHAT?

Just where should fiscal responsibility lie? Several observers point out that the computer center or service is as likely to have expertise in these areas as the library:

> Since resources have flowed to the computer centers of the world, it is logical that much of the initiative, guidance, and modeling has fallen to these as well. If libraries do not have control over their infrastructure, how can they have service control? This is a major implication of the new financial realities as the profession moves into new technologies.[4]

There is often a lack of coordination between the decision-making of the library administrator and the decision-making of the overall financial controller in an institution and, downstream, between the financial controller and the user. Rather than engage in territorial struggle, a smart library will seek to integrate its decision-making processes through computer services and to achieve consensus on respective responsibilities. In Davenport's 1992 survey of accounting practice in campuses in the UK, a common solution was to assign responsibility for the running of services to the library as a cost center, and for connectivity and equipment to the computer center or its equivalent.[5] In some cases, users were able to determine their own information budget at departmental level. Though the data in that survey is now only of historic value (there have been changes in infrastructure with a move to block purchase of networked services by the UK's Bath Information and Data Service and other similar agencies on behalf a group of subscribing institutions) this general division of labor still holds in many cases, though recently the UK government funded e-Lib program, has established pilot projects for the provision of electronic documents which test, along with other management issues in the digital library, a range of costing models.

We stress throughout our text that fiscal matters in any library are now the domain of staff units that are increasing in size and diversity, and that finding out who needs to know what is as important as mastery of accounting techniques and procedures. The following checklist from Hayes and Brown will be of use to any service planner:

- Is centralization an issue?
- If any of the staff make financial decisions, are they also informed of the library's budget and financial priorities?
- If many people are involved in financial planning, are there sufficient auditing, security and control systems in place to ensure the effective working of the library?
- Obversely, are there so many controls and/or paperwork trails that the library isn't able to function properly?
- Does anyone within or related to the library system have independent authority and responsibility?
- When financial relationships are mapped, is it necessary to change any of them to those relationships and workflow?[6]

BASIC FINANCIAL ANALYSIS FOR LIBRARY MANAGERS

Given the scope of the concerns and doubts and fears of practitioners, we believe that there is a clear need for enlightenment in the area of financial, managerial and cost accounting. The emphasis in our text is on teaching practitioners how to manage finances for electronic systems and services. This means teaching them how to come up with reasonably accurate numbers for the amount of money they will have to spend in order to be able to institute services, run/operate them and price them. We will show how different kinds of information about costs may be combined and classified, using established categories, to show how money is spent on electronic systems.

The concepts that you need to grasp in order to effectively cost and price and financially manage are inter-related and you need to be familiar with all of them in order to understand what costing is. Though we explain them linearly at this stage, remember that they are not mutually exclusive.

BASIC CONCEPTS

Cash flow

There will be a difference between what accountants record, and what you actually do with information for planning purposes. What you as a manager are concerned with is the control of resources, in this case, monetary resources; and to do this, you have to know how they behave. You must be able to answer such questions as: 'What is the movement of resources at particular times?' and 'When do transactions occur?' Another important question is what distinguishes expenses and assets. The essence of this is timing – you must identify the point at which resources actually leave the organization.

To handle all of this, the first concept with which a manager has to be familiar is cash flow: a self-explanatory term – the movement of cash within an organization from the moment it enters to the moment it leaves that organization. Cash flow is extremely important because, of all the resources that are needed to run an organization effectively, cash is normally the one that is in most short supply. People often confuse cash flow with revenue and expense; the difference is that an expense is cash of which you actually lose the value as it flows out of the organization. An expense occurs if there has been a loss of resources.

Cash flow, then, is the movement of cash resources in or out of the organization that occurs when (say) I write a check for $50 for the electric bill or $1000 for the computer (cash resources flow out); or a patron pays me $200 or a customer gives me $500 for online searches (cash resources flow in). Cash flow is concerned with the availability of funds in an organization and this is important from the managerial standpoint because the ability to conduct transactions is a fundamental element of being able to manage. Remember that expense and revenue are not synonymous with cash flow.

For any analyst, cash flows are the interesting thing in controlling funds, as management of cash flows has direct operational implications. The management of transactions derives not only from an understanding of what happens when assets leave the organization, but also from an understanding of the nature of assets that you have. This understanding allows you to assess the scope for action that your assets afford you, and provides a realistic assessment of what you can do with them.

Assets

An asset is defined as the resources which the organization enjoys or expects to get benefit from in the future. The concept of future benefit is particularly important because it is that idea that distinguishes assets from expenses – the timing when benefits are received is an important criterion.

For example, you spend $1200 on a computer: the machine has an estimated life of three years. When you make the transaction, in this case, there is a cash flow out of the organization of $1200; however, the resources have not left. So you must always ask: when do the resources actually leave the organization?

One way to approach this question is to divide cost by effective life in years. Thus, for each of the three years of the computer's life, $400 of resources has left the organization. This is called straight-line depreciation. There are other ways of describing depreciation; in this case, $400 per year marks the fact that value is leaving, but this does not represent an additional loss of operating funds. Remember that depreciation does not affect cash flow in subsequent years – in other words, cash and value are not the same.

Liabilities

Liabilities are defined as any legal claim against the assets of an organization. Imagine, then, that you buy your $1200 computer with a credit loan rather than cash. At the time you take delivery of your computer, there is no cash flow, but the seller has a legal claim against your assets for $1200 – if you did not pay, they could take steps to recover their money. Here, if you assume you are paying for your computer at the rate of $100 a month with no interest payments, every month $100 flows out of the organization which reduces its liability; but you do not gain additional value; all you are doing is reducing your obligations.

Expenses

Expenses are defined generally as an outflow of resource which is attached to a particular period in time – usually the current operating year. They are resources which have no future value – only a current value. Thus, you receive an electricity bill for $100 the month of May: you have consumed electricity and paid for it and there is no expectation of future value.

In the case of our computer example, the initial cash payment of $1200 was merely a transaction whereby one asset was traded for another of equal value – the expense in this case (i.e. the outflow for which there is no future value) – occurs for each year as we depreciate it: a depreciation expense of $400 per annum. This is a recognition that an outflow of resources for a particular period occurs. The key again is timing – when does the outflow occur? If it is in the current year it is an expense; if it will occur in the future, not in the current year, it is an asset. After one year, we still have $800 of assets. (There are conventions which allow us to decide when the flow of resources actually occurs. Readers interested in a more detailed discussion of depreciation techniques and in the application of depreciation specifically to libraries are referred to Horngren.[7])

Revenue

Revenue is an in-flow of resources into an organization. It is straightforward in most not-for-profits organizations such as libraries where managers are supplied with operating funds. One important feature of revenue receipt in a not-for profit organization where funds are received before the goods or services are provided is that whoever provides those funds has a legitimate claim against the monies they have given you. You as a manager cannot recognize them as revenue until you have spent them in ways that the organizational commitment says you have to. Thus, for example, if a business customer provides you with $500 to do online searching for the next year, that money is treated as a liability until the online searching for which that money has paid for has taken place. You as a manager took the money with a specific obligation to provide some service – it only becomes revenue when or as you provide that service.

Cost

Costs may be defined as the value of resources exchanged either for future or current benefits. Thus the term 'cost' is used in ways that may not appear consistent – in some cases, it is synonymous with expense; in other situations, it refers to the outflow of resources in exchange for assets. Thus costing a service can mean deciding what the investment of funds will be, not only on a yearly basis but also with regard to the purchase of assets. In this text, we will make it clear when we mean one thing or the other but you may find, however, that the business community may vary in the way it uses the word 'costs'. In Chapter 2, we look at costs in more detail.

ACCOUNTING TERMS

At a basic level, you as a manager must be able to speak and understand the professional language of an 'expert' when you have to deal with a professional accountant. Accounting takes costs and attaches them to specific periods of time as they move out of the organization. There are different ways of doing this and we will review them briefly as follows.

Financial accounting

Financial accounting is a term which refers to the public reporting and disclosure of financial records according to a variety of professional and legal standards. These standards specify how and for what expenses may be recognized, where on an income statement they are lodged, and so on. Financial accounting is used for external reporting and is consistent across organizations.

Cost accounting

Cost accounting is a form of modeling which, if it conforms to established practice, remains constant across different activities, programs and institutions. Bryson (1990) observes that 'Cost accounting is not an end in itself. It is used to determine if the resources have been used effectively'.[8]

Cost accounting, according to Bryson, can be used in libraries to determine the anticipated value of certain activities, and for comparative purposes to measure efficiency. It is the simple process of breaking down resources associated with a particular activity, and then collating the results to show the monetary cost of that activity. In libraries, the practice falls into two categories: routine costing which is used to provide regular financial and management information; and special exercise costing, which deals with specific projects.

Routine cost-output or cost-activity ratios are used on a comparative basis to measure the efficiencies of certain library functions, cost centers or services. By themselves these ratios serve no real purpose but when they are used to compare branch libraries within a system, or to make external comparisons between similar types of organizations (for example), they provide valuable management information.

Special costing exercises are concerned with particular activities or groups of activities; they are used to address specific issues such as a comparison between the current cost of operations and the estimated costs of alternative methods. It is important to remember that the costs relating to proposed systems need to be related not only to existing systems, but also to the other benefits which will result. It may well be that a new system is approved not so much on the grounds of costs savings alone but also on the benefits and improvements of the new service to the user it may offer.

In a distributed environment, a portable costing method will be extremely useful if a manager is likely to be concerned with financial liaison across a number of institutions or branches. On the supply side, the electronic market offers a rich array of competing services and products: compatibility in costing and pricing will be a strong selling point in the eyes of buyers who may have to mix and match across vendors. On the demand side, many institutions purchase services and products as members of consortia, and in both the UK and the US there are moves to scale up consortial activity and finance parts of both academic and public service from regional cost centers. In such cases, the costs of participation in consortial ventures may be an important part of fiscal management.

Internal audit

In addition to routine and special reporting, cost accounting is also used for the purposes of internal audit. Smith (1989) demonstrates how it can be used to measure management efficiency and managerial integrity.[9] We return briefly to this subject in our last chapter where we suggest that an internal audit can validate good financial judgment and expose incompetence.

Managerial accounting

Managerial accounting refers primarily to financial information supplied to managers so that they may make decisions about the organization in which they work. The way this information is provided may vary across organizations. Cost accounting has to a large extent been subsumed by managerial accounting. Traditionally, cost accounting has involved the accumulation and allocation of costs to departments and units of products with the aim of costing products for inventory purposes and for determining income. In current usage, cost accounting often refers to the gathering and allocation of costs, in an organizational policy-setting context, for any activity about which management needs to make decisions, including routine valuation of the services it provides, and non-routine decisions such as adding or reducing services.

Though such distinctions may be historically important, a library administrator or manager does not need to dwell on them as they are unlikely to be crucial to decision-making. The approach that this book takes is pragmatic in that it discusses concepts from the perspective of their utility in making decisions rather than their historical provenance, and it is important that you understand that there may be conventions for reporting and other legal requirements in public accounting that this book does not attempt to address. We are concerned to help you, as readers and managers, to make good decisions for planning, control and investment. It is not our primary intention to prepare you to produce financial statements that show strict adherence to accounting reporting protocols, as other texts cover this ground.[10]

PLANNING AND CONTROL

One of the primary reasons for gathering and analyzing cost information is to assist management in planning and controlling the operations of an organization. There are numerous definitions of planning and control but for the purposes of this text we define planning as the process of formulating organizational goals and assessing the potential outcomes of various ways of achieving those goals. Control is the process of implementing the goals and evaluating the effectiveness with which they are achieved.

Managers should be aware that decisions are, and should be, based on a range of criteria that include but are not restricted to finance. For example, a public library might perform 200 online searches per year at an average cost of $20 per search (total costs of $4000). The library board may elect, however, to offer the search at a reduced fee of $5 or even at no charge because they feel that public benefit of the service warrants offering it at a financial loss to the library. This is not to say, however, that cost information was not useful in the decision. Understanding the cost of offering the system assists the library managers in three ways:

1 Knowing the costs of the service it provides allows the library to make better-informed decisions about whether to offer that service. If the yearly costs to the library were $40,000 rather than $4000, subsidizing the searches might be less desirable or even economically impossible.

2 Being aware of the total cost of the service alerts the library to the need for finding the money from other funds and sources within the organization.

3 The presence of cost information provides evidence of a thoughtful decision even in cases where the decision is to provide a service that loses money. Much of the financial information provided by organizations is often used by those organizations for rhetorical purposes. Those such as granting agencies or higher levels of management within an organization or local government committees like to see evidence that their money is well spent. Evidence of competent stewardship of funds is a strong motivator for receiving funds in the future. Organizations or departments who appear competent in handling money are more likely to receive continued or increased funds in the future.

THE PHILOSOPHY OF PLANNING AND ESTIMATING FOR ELECTRONIC RESOURCES

The biggest problem when we try to manage a systems project is the organizational resistance to planning and estimation. Managers of all sorts are usually under enormous pressure to act – when the time comes to make decisions about systems and services, the first thing that people want to do is to be seen to be busy and to be achieving goals and what this generally means is that people do not bother with planning and estimating first. There is a prevailing attitude that it is too difficult or too inaccurate to make estimates about systems and that it is not productive to make plans and estimates. In some cases, a 'snap' decision may have to be made, as in the case where residual funds have to be spent before the end of the financial year.

The costs and benefits of financial reporting systems or other evaluative projects, can be evaluated and estimated like any other costs and benefits. A finance reporting system is a commodity that has to be paid for just like copy or paper; all of them should be evaluated in terms of whether they provide information that is more valuable to management than the expense it takes to collect and produce it. As a rule of thumb, the greater the implications, the greater the evaluation efforts must be. Systems and services that require great commitment or other kinds of of managerial exposure, should be worth a greater investment in information gathering; some decisions will not require the same level of input as others. Any planning and evaluation and estimation is better than none: what is fatal is ignorance. Take the time to think of the things you should be mindful of in a project, even a project carried out at short notice. The following (true) parable illustrates the point.

COMMON FALLACIES ABOUT PLANNING

SCENARIO

Jean runs a gallery of calligraphic art that holds regular exhibitions for which expensive catalogues are needed. She came up with what appeared to be a good idea for cutting costs. Breathless with excitement she called her systems analysis friend to share her insights.

Jean: 'I've had the most marvelous idea for cutting catalogue costs. I'm going to set up a hypercard stack on a computer in the gallery so people can click on images and get information about the artist or calligrapher and background documentation about calligraphic art as well as the exhibits. The best thing is that I've got four weeks before the next show to set it up.'

Systems analyst: *'Have you sat down and thought about everything that needs to happen before you can set this up, and how well it will work? Go talk to your computer programmer and tell him what you want to do and if you still decide that you want to go through with it I'll buy you dinner at the best restaurant in town.'*

A day later Jean called back somewhat sheepishly.

Jean: *'I guess you win. It turns out that the only computer that we have doesn't run particularly fast and my programmer estimates that it will take at least a minute to switch from one image to another. There's only one electrical outlet to plug the machine into, and that isn't even in the gallery – it's in the hall outside. I have over two hundred people coming to the opening, can you imagine the back-up? I'm getting off lightly with paying for your dinner'.*

This scenario illustrates several common fallacies. Fallacy one is that 'System quality is all that matters'. This is usually expressed as: 'The system will be so cool everybody will want to use it.' Not so. Experience shows that no matter how good the technology is:

- The system will fail if it's not the solution you need;
- It can still cost too much or be implemented too late to be of use;
- People won't use it if you don't convince them they need to.

Fallacy two is that 'No projections are better than inaccurate projections'. This is usually expressed as: 'Come on. The whole project is so complicated with so much stuff to take into account nobody could do it. We'll be so far off base anyway what's the use of even trying?' Not so. Remember:

- Who says estimates have to be perfect? They're a guideline. You can revise and amend them. At least they offer a process for ordered development that makes you look at things like cost, time, users, and things like that.

Fallacy three is that you can 'Skip the planning when you're in a hurry'. This is usually expressed as: 'What – are you nuts? We only have six weeks to make this fly, and you want me to write up reports? I don't think that's very helpful of you.' Not so:

- Without a plan you can actually waste time. You have to correct mistakes, put things in you left out, and you may even have to junk the system that you built too quickly anyway.

Strictly speaking, these are not financial considerations, but it is important to realize that what drives financial projections is an acknowledgment of risk and uncertainty. The key to successful planning is to build allowances for risk and uncertainty into your plans and projections. We look at this in Chapter 4.

To conclude the chapter, we offer you two exercises that will allow you to test your ability to classify resources in different contexts. The first asks you to use basic concepts of financial accounting; and the second, to gather information and make planning decisions.

EXERCISE ONE: WHAT DO I HAVE?

Background

Mega Library has decided to install an online public access catalog (OPAC). The equipment for the system including the central processing unit (CPU) and the associated peripheral hardware (terminals, printers, etc.) costs $50,000. It has an estimated life of four years. In order to install the equipment the library needs to upgrade its electrical system. The improvements to the electrical system will become a permanent part of the building. This work will cost $15,000. The terminals are connected via fiber optic cables which need to be run in conduits through utility tunnels run under the floor. The cost of the cables and their installation is $15,000.

During the course of installation, asbestos is found in the ceiling tiles which costs an additional $5000 to remove. When the entire installation is nearly complete an occupational health inspector visits and announces that the air in the computer room is unfit for humans to breathe and that improved ventilation is needed. These improvements cost an additional and unexpected $10,000. In order to set the system up for public use, the library purchases new public work stations which costs $4000.

During the time that the system is being implemented, five of the library staff are sent away for training in order to become proficient in running the OPAC. The total training costs for the staff amount to $2000, with an additional $600 for travel costs. The total salaries for the employees who run the OPAC are $80,000 per year.

The library pays four firms for licensing software. Three of the firms require yearly payments of $500, $750 and $400 respectively. The fourth licenses software only for periods of three years for which it charges $600 in total.

During the first year of operation, the library spends $2000 on paper, printer ribbons and related office supplies. Electricity charges for running both the OPAC system and the additional ventilation system are $2000 for the first year.

Once the OPAC is running, a second library in the community contracts with Mega Library to gain access to its OPAC. This contract brings in $4500 for three years of access.

Questions
How should each of the sums expended by Mega Library be categorized in terms of:

1   assets;
2   liabilities;
3   expenses;
4   revenues?

Sample answers
1   The equipment used in the OPAC including the terminals, CPU and workstations are all assets. A library, in most cases, would buy all this equipment with the expectation that it would have a life span longer than one year. In such cases, the full value of the purchased item is not received during its first year of ownership. It must therefore be treated as an asset. For each year of the asset's life a portion of its purchase price is deducted and treated as a depreciation expense in recognition of the fact that it is worth less as time progresses. If we assume a three-year life for the computer equipment the yearly values and expenses would appear as follows:

	$
Equipment	50,000
Public work stations	4,000
Total cost of equipment and work stations	54,000

	Remaining value of assets ($)	Depreciation expense for year ($)
Year 1	36,000	18,000
Year 2	18,000	18,000
Year 3	0	18,000

As we noted earlier, cash (represented by the amount of the full price of the equipment) flows out of the library at the time of purchase. However, this cash is given in exchange for other assets of equal value, so that there is no net outflow of resources. In this example an outflow of resources is recognized only with the yearly recording of a depreciation expense, although there is no additional outflow of cash.

2   Improvements and modifications made to the library in order to install the OPAC and provide a safe working space are all treated as assets. In each case, the improvements form a part of the library building and provide benefits in the future as well as in the year in which the library pays for them.

	$
Electrical work	15,000
Cables and installation	15,000
Asbestos removal	5,000
Ventilation system	10,000

The payment of $4500 to Mega Library from a second library is a liability until Mega actually provides access. Mega accepted the money in the expectation that it would provide future access to its OPAC so that if Mega does not provide the access as agreed, the second library is able to claim its money back. Over time, as Mega provides access and fulfills its obligations, these funds become revenue. As in the case of depreciation, the flow of cash occurs during the first year of the transaction. The subsequent recognition of a portion of the liability as revenue does not result in additional cash flowing into Mega Library's accounts.

3   The cost of training provided for Mega's employees and the associated travel costs are normally treated as an expense. It is true that the library is likely to gain future benefit for the employees, but there is no logical way to calculate the value or effective life of personal information, neither can the library guarantee that it will maintain possession of the training since an employee may leave at any time. Thus, these costs are usually categorized as an expense:

	$
Staff training costs	2,000
Travel cost for training	600

4 The following amounts should also be treated as expenses:

	$
Salaries	80,000
Office supplies	2,000
Utilities	2,000
Software licenses	1,850 (500+750+400+200)

Salaries, office supplies, utilities and yearly licensing fees are all (specifically cash) outflows of resources which are for benefits received only during the current year. An exception to this is the license for the fourth software supplier. The $600 paid to the supplier is for three years of use. Therefore, only $200 of this amount is treated as an expense (assuming straight-line depreciation) since the other $400 is for benefits that the library will not receive until the second and third years of software use.

EXERCISE TWO: TO JOIN OR NOT TO JOIN?

Background
Arthur Smith is Director of the Mega Library's Technical Services Department. During his mid-morning break he unburdened himself to a colleague.

'I'm going to have to increase my dosage of Prozac if I don't make this decision soon. We've been offered the opportunity to join the XYZ regional cataloging cooperative. The yearly fee to belong is $26,000 for a library of our size, but in return they can provide at least 85% of our cataloging needs. I think it may free a librarian for other duties and so I may even be able to save some money if we join. It has to be cheaper to catalog this way at some level, but I have no idea how much. I have no idea what it costs us to catalog. For all I know we may only spend $20,000 on cataloging so joining would be a financial disaster. There's no way I can find out how much we spend on cataloging, there're so many things involved in the process. I'm just going to have to guess about it. Maybe I'll flip a coin. I don't see any way that the decision can be any worse that way. What do you think I should do?'

Questions
1 If you were in charge of financial management at Mega Library, what

issues needing more detailed investigation and analysis should you address in order to improve the quality of the decision Arthur has to make?

2 What are the likely benefits to Mega Library if Arthur decides to join?

Sample answers

1 What kinds of issues do you need to gather information about? Firstly, the financial costs attached to either option. If the Financial Director claims that he or she has no idea, this is unlikely to be true. The first issue is: How much financial exposure is attached to either option? What will be the strength of the commitment in money or other terms? If Mega Library will only have to pay $100 per year to join the consortium, the problem is trivial and the effort to gather information is not worth it. If a more significant investment is involved, ask what is the commitment in terms of time: for how long will the decision be binding – one year or more? If the commitment is long-term, it may be difficult to foresee adverse consequences.

  If a non-trivial decision to join or not to join is to be made, the manager will have to gather cost information, and should be able to provide even a rough estimate. If the proposed genuinely cannot be costed, it may be too risky.

2 Next, you will need to establish the likely benefits. What do you hope to achieve by adopting the proposed course of action? Cost savings? Improved service quality? Or both? No matter what the level of improvement might be, if it will cost say $50,000 and the budget is $40,000, the commitment cannot be made as the library has finite resources to expend.

REFERENCES

1   Robinson, B. M. and Robinson, S., 'Strategic planning and program budgeting for libraries', *Library trends*, **42** (3), 1994, 420–7.

2   Dunn, J. A. and Martin, M.S., 'The whole cost of libraries', *Library trends*, **42** (3), 1994, 564–78.

3   *Op. cit.*

4   Hayes, S. and Brown, D., 'The library as a business: mapping the pervasiveness of financial relationships in today's library', *Library trends*, **42** (3), 1994, 404–19

5   Davenport, E., 'Accounting for networked services: a preliminary report'. In *Proceedings of the 18th International Online Information Meeting*, Oxford, Learned Information, 1994, 393–403.

6   Hayes and Brown, *op. cit.*

7 Horngren, C. T., *Cost accounting: a managerial emphasis*, Englewood Cliffs, NJ., Prentice Hall, 1982.

8 Bryson, J., 'Budgeting and economic analysis'. In *Effective library and information centre management*, London, Gower, 1990, 345–73.

9 Smith, S., *Managerial accounting for librarians and other not-for-profit managers*, Chicago, IL., American Library Association, 1991.

10 McKay, D., *Effective financial planning for library and information services*, London, Aslib, 1995.

CHAPTER 2

Finding costs

The purpose of this chapter is to acquaint the library manager with the concepts and methods needed to identify the costs that go into an electronic service or system. In order to do this, the manager must be able to determine the types of cost that relate to the system, the intervals at which they will be paid, and how these costs change with changes in levels of activity. Later chapters will discuss techniques for combining costs, estimating the cost of systems over time, and making decisions for prices and investments. The foundation of any sound financial decision-making technique, however, must be the most accurate reckoning possible of the likely cost of the system under consideration. As with any other decision, the garbage in – garbage out principle applies: the decisions we make concerning the purchase and installation of electronic systems will only be as good as the cost information on which those decisions are based.

SCENARIO

Last year, Mega Library installed an online searching system and began running database searches for local businesses and individuals. The service proved to be very popular and a neighboring library suggested that Mega Library should conduct searches for them on a fee-for-service basis. Mega Library's Director conducted some preliminary cost analyses and determined that the connect time and the appropriate part of a searcher's salary would cost $50 per search. 'I know we're not using all the system's capacity,' he said to his system manager, 'So I don't see why we can't take on additional searches as long as the other libraries pay their way.'

He then negotiated a contract with the neighboring library to conduct searches for $52 per search with an expected additional volume of 800 searches. 'We should be able to cover our costs and *generate some good-will besides,' he said. 'I've added a bit more to the cost-of-search figure and we may even be able to turn a small profit if we charge the service out at that rate.'*

Six months later we find him at his desk, looking very harried. 'I don't understand what happened. We've ended up having to buy a new machine to handle all the new online search requests. The fees don't begin to cover the costs and now we're going to lose thousands. I don't see how it could have happened. I'm sure the costs I worked out were correct.'

IDENTIFYING AND UNDERSTANDING COSTS

The problem in this case is not, unfortunately, rare. The difference between identifying and understanding costs is often the difference between making wise and unwise decisions about systems and services. Many of the costs that go into an automated system are not immediately obvious and there is a real risk that an inexperienced manager will overlook some of them and under-cost it. Moreover, not all workplace costs are treated in the same way so that comparing them may involve more than a simple additive process.

In order to identify accurately the costs that comprise a system, we need to begin by understanding:

1   basic definitions of cost concepts;
2   how costs behave in a work environment; and
3   which costs to include in an electronic system.

This chapter will begin by discussing these concepts generally and then incorporating them into an actual work example involving connecting a workplace to the Internet.

COSTING TERMINOLOGY

As discussed in Chapter 1, accounting, like any other discipline, has its own jargon and it may be helpful to remind you of some of the terms used by accountants to describe costs before we discuss the behavior of costs. The glossary at the end of the book provides further explanations of a range of relevant terms.

Costs

As we saw earlier, costs are resources (expressed in terms of cash value) that have been exchanged for goods or services with the expectation that those goods or services will produce future value. As the benefits those costs have bought are realized, the costs are said to 'expire'. Expired costs are defined as expenses. Unexpired costs (costs which are still expected to produce future benefits) are defined as assets.

Cost objective

Anything within an organization whose cost needs to be measured is a **cost objective**. Costs are an important component of record-keeping in organizations, but they are not collected for their own sake. Costs are gathered and evaluated for the purpose of guiding managerial decisions. Therefore, costs need to be 'about' something and this 'something' is the cost objective. A cost objective may be the running of a reference desk, an online search performed for a customer, setting up a LAN, or any other activity of managerial interest. Cost objectives may be activities over which a manager has control, but control is not a necessary characteristic of a cost objective.

Cost centers

Areas of responsibility in which a manager is accountable for incurring costs are called **cost centers**. A reference department may be a cost center, for example, if its director has the responsibility for controlling the costs of providing a reference service. A cost center might also be a revenue center if its manager also controls the inflow of funds through making marketing and pricing decisions. A cost center may have any number of cost objectives. In order to understand cost objectives and make better managerial decisions (in some cases to better manage cost centers), we need to gather cost information and understand how costs behave.

HOW COSTS BEHAVE IN A WORK ENVIRONMENT

Fixed and variable costs

Costs are categorized as **fixed** or **variable** according to the ways in which they change with changes in activity levels. Activities may be measured in a number of ways including operating time, individuals served, questions answered, searches performed, etc. A cost is variable if it changes directly in proportion to fluctuations in an activity. A cost is fixed if it remains unchanged despite fluctuations in activity levels.

We may illustrate the difference by referring back to Mega Library and its search service. For each online search that Mega Library performs, it incurs one hour of a searcher's time and 20 minutes of connect time, payable to an online vendor. Since both these costs vary in relation to the number of searches performed, they are variable. If, however, Mega Library instead leases a computer terminal on an annual basis at a cost of $2,000 annually, irrespective of the number of searches Mega Library makes on the computer, that cost would be a fixed cost.

Fixed costs and the relevant range

Accountants sometimes point out that all costs are variable in the long term since an organization may go out of business and default on its payments. This is an extreme position, but it demonstrates the need for managers to be aware that fixed costs do not remain fixed for an indefinite period of time or range of activities. A fixed cost only remains fixed for a limited range of activity or time known as the **relevant range**. Let us assume that Mega Library leases a computer for online searching for $20,000 a year. The computer has a maximum searching capacity of 2200 searches per year. At any level of searching between 0 and 2200 searches, the library will continue to pay the yearly lease fee of $20,000. If, however, demand for searches increases to 3000 searches a year it will be necessary to purchase a new computer. The fixed cost for leases thus increases to $40,000 a year.

Mixed costs

Mixed costs are defined as costs that exhibit properties both of fixed and variable costs. Telephone charges are an example in that customers typically pay a fixed amount (e.g. $50 a month) simply to have a telephone connection, regardless of the volume of calls made. In addition, they pay additional amounts based on the number of minutes of calling time (e.g. $0.50 a minute). A company that averaged 200 minutes of calling would therefore incur a monthly telephone bill of $150, of which $100 (200 minutes @ $0.50 a minute) was variable and $50.00 was fixed.

WHY THE CONCERN WITH CATEGORIZING FIXED AND VARIABLE COSTS?

Managers frequently have to make decisions to add new services or reduce existing ones. By not understanding the makeup and behavior of costs related to that service, a manager may underestimate the cost of increasing the level of a service or overestimate the savings to be made by cutting it. Let us return to Mega Library's online search service and see how this works.

WORKED EXAMPLE: COSTS OF A SEARCH

To conduct a single search in Mega Library we incur the following variable costs:

	$
I hour of searcher's time @$10/hour	10
20 minutes of connect time @$2/minute	40
Total variable cost for a single search	50

These costs are variable since they increase directly in proportion to the number of searches that are made: one search costs $50, 100 searches cost $5000 ($50 × 100), etc.

	$
Yearly lease cost for one computer	20,000

This cost is fixed since the library pays the $20,000 regardless of how many searches they make on it (up to the capacity of the computer).

WORKED EXAMPLE: COSTS OF SEARCHES FOR OUTSIDE CLIENTS

Let us assume for this example that the library currently performs 1800 searches each year. The library Director recognizes that this is below the system's capacity (but doesn't recognize that the fixed costs have a relevant range) and agrees to provide searches for a neighboring library for a fee of $52 a search. The resulting demand for searches at this price is an additional 800 searches per year for Mega Library.

The Director has incorrectly assumed the following cost behavior:

Before the additional searches:

	$
Variable search costs	
1800 searches @ $50	90,000
Fixed costs	20,000
Total yearly search costs	110,000

With the addition of the other library's searches:

	$
Variable search costs	
2600 searches @ $50	130,000
Fixed costs	20,000
Less revenue from library 2	
800 searches @ $52.00	(41,600)
Total net cost to Mega Library	108,400

In fact, the correct costs to the library should look like this:

	$
Variable search costs	
2600 searches @ $50	130,000
	$
Total fixed costs	
$20,000 + $20,000	40,000
(an additional computer is needed to handle greater volume of searches)	
Less revenue from library 2	
800 searches @ $52	(41,600)
Total net cost to Mega Library	128,400

The additional searches actually end up costing Mega Library more money rather than generating a savings. Conversely, programs cannot be cut below the level of their fixed costs. If Mega Library's

Director had decided to offer these additional services, the library would still have incurred $40,000 in fixed expenses even if it performed no online searching.

DIRECT AND INDIRECT COSTS

Direct costs are those costs that can be traced to a particular cost objective. However, organizations also have **indirect costs**, sometimes known as **overheads**, which are common to a range of cost objectives and cannot be easily and directly traced to any single one of them.

Administrative costs are a common example of indirect costs. In order to run a computer system someone must order supplies, produce paychecks for the system operators, pay the utility bills that power the building, etc. The labor and material costs necessary to undertake these tasks are seldom connected directly to running the system, since an administrative office usually performs these tasks for the entire organization, but it is also clear that the system cannot run without them. Similar examples of overhead costs might be janitor salaries, cleaning supplies, building repairs, etc.

Allocating indirect costs

A fundamental problem in determining the costs of systems or services is deciding what proportion of indirect costs should be assigned to the total costs of the system or services. The process of making the decision is referred to in accounting terms as **cost allocation**. In a general sense, cost allocation may defined as assigning the costs from one cost objective to other cost objectives. Costs may be allocated for a variety of managerial purposes including decisions to add new services, evaluating managerial performance, encouraging or discouraging the use of organizational resources such as computers or maintenance and setting prices or justifying costs. As a general rule, there are three steps for allocating costs:

1   Select a cost objective to which indirect costs will be allocated. Normally such objectives are services, products or departments.

2   Collect the range of indirect costs (typically known as a costs pool) that are associated with a particular cost objective.
3   Select some method (usually referred to as an allocation base) for connecting the costs in (2) with the objective in (1). A typical base for allocating overhead is direct labor hours.

The ideal base is one that serves as the cause for incurring indirect costs. Unfortunately, it is often difficult to find strong cause and effect relationships in service environments. In such cases the criterion for choosing a base should be associative. That is, you should ask whether a change in the base acts as an accurate predictor for the total costs of the cost objective even if there is no logical basis for a causal relationship.

Why are indirect costs important?

The decision as to which costs to allocate and the method of allocating them can have implications for the pricing of services or the control of costs by managers.

> **WORKED EXAMPLE: EXTERNAL CLIENT SERVICES**
>
> Mega Library calculates that each online search that it performs requires $10 of direct labor and $8 of direct connect time. If an outside business asks the library to perform online searches on a fee for service basis, Mega might price the service at $18 per search since that covers the direct costs of the service. At the same time, however, Mega cannot provide an online searching service without administrative staff to run the library, utility costs to control the temperature of the library, the fixed cost of purchasing the computers that perform the search, or the mortgage payments that house the service. The library management might argue that, since an online search is impossible without incurring the above overhead costs, and other costs, it would be reasonable to expect the client business to pay a proportion of them.
>
> This is not to suggest that one pricing strategy is necessarily better than the other, only that knowledge of the total costs and the strategies for allocating them better informs the pricing decision.

WORKED EXAMPLE: OUTSOURCING

A related example might involve a departmental decision to outsource its computer maintenance. Imagine a computer maintenance department with total yearly costs of $30,000. Of this amount, $5000 is attributed to the reference department. The reference department contracts with a maintenance vendor to provide service for the sum of $4100 per year. The bulk of the maintenance department's costs are fixed, however, and the department has its yearly costs drop only to $29,000. As result the entire library has incurred an additional, outside, expense of $4100 with an internal savings of only $1000. Thus the entire library spends an additional $3100 rather than experiencing the $900 savings that the reference manager imagines he achieved.

The issues relating to and techniques for allocating costs are sufficiently complex and important to require a more detailed treatment and this is provided in Chapter 3, which concerns assigning costs to cost centers.

SUNK COSTS

Sunk costs are costs for which an outlay has already been made and which cannot be affected by any current decisions. An example of a sunk cost might be the non-refundable purchase of a computer for $5000. Sunk costs, and indeed historical costs of any sort, have no validity as the basis for making future decisions although they may be the best (or only) predictor of future costs. We will revisit the concept of sunk costs in Chapter 4, which deals with investment decisions.

DECIDING HOW COSTS BEHAVE

In this chapter and throughout the text we make the point that correctly understanding the behavior of costs can make the difference between wise and unwise management decisions. Unfortunately, real cost data is messy to work with and difficult to use in predicting future events. You may find two assumptions widely used by accountants useful when making cost estimates for electronic systems or indeed for any product, system or service:

1   the total cost level should be expressed as a single independent
    variable such as hours of search time rather than by a combina-
    tion of several variables such as number of searches, databases
    used
2   linear approximations of variable costs are accurate enough even
    though costs are more likely to behave nonlinearly.

For the purposes of cost calculations of the level described in this
book, rough approximations based on these assumptions will usually
be good enough. Library managers can usually estimate the behavior of the cost components of their automation systems by setting
the expected changes in price against expected levels of activity.
Managers are cautioned, however, that it is usually possible to predict changes in activity levels reliably only within a relevant range of
activities.

In practical terms, managers need to classify costs according to
the control that they have over the behavior of these costs. A good
example of this is electric power: electricity is a classic example, in
theory, of a variable cost in that the cost of electricity varies directly
with the number of kilowatts per hour consumed. In practice, however, a manager may have very little control over the consumption
of electricity. For example, a library may close several days each
week in order to cut expenses, but it is unlikely that electric consumption will drop to zero since power is still needed to heat the
building, run the security system, operate the parking lot lights, etc.
The drop, in fact, may be quite small given the relative power consumption of such activities. Similarly, electricity may be included as
part of the overhead allocated to a department, in which case, the
department has no real operational control over its power consumption.

Gathering cost information

An important consideration for managers in regard to gathering cost
information is that the historical activity bases used in an organization may not be useful in making managerial decisions. For example,
it is common in many libraries to keep track of costs according to

physical locations such as branch libraries or to functional areas, such as technical services. Automation services, however, frequently cut across physical and departmental lines. In such cases, it may be necessary to gather new cost information that relate to activities.

Gathering cost information is also not strictly a financial operation. Instead, it is a set of managerial decisions that should be based on an understanding of what an automated system needs to accomplish. It is strongly recommended that a thorough systems analysis be performed first to ensure that the automated system selected actually performs the task that the organization needs.

Librarians should be prepared to be involved in the systems analysis process and to be willing to ask questions about the price of the system's components for various levels of service. Remember, once a system has been purchased, most of its operating costs will be out of your control. The key to obtaining a cost-effective automated system is to become involved early.

If we are prepared to become involved in the process of planning for automated systems, what costs should we look at? This question may seem obvious until you realize that many assets that provide similar levels of operational service may have widely divergent purchase and operating costs. Fax machines are a good example of this. At the present time, purchasers of fax machines can choose between machines that use plain paper and machines that use thermal sensitive paper. The purchase price of plain paper machines is significantly greater than that of thermal paper machines, perhaps by a factor of two to three. They are, however, significantly cheaper to operate since they do not need special (and consequently more expensive) paper.

Thus, an office that handles many faxes during the course of a day might spend a significant amount of money during the course of a year on special fax paper. Depending on the volume of faxes generated and the cost of the paper, the increased operating cost could easily outweigh any savings in the initial purchase price. The situation is complicated by the fact that the quality of a sheet of thermal fax paper may vary over time: in a year's time it may be nothing more than a sheet of gray paper. An office that needs to retain faxes for archival purposes must then photocopy all its faxes, further adding to its costs.

The point of this example is to illustrate that there's often much more to costs than the simple purchase price of an asset. An organization's commitment to an asset grows over time and assets with relatively cheap purchase costs can often have significant additional costs over time. Since most of these costs are built in at the time we acquire an asset, we need to consider them *before* we make the decision to purchase. Managers sometimes cite the difficulties of estimating any cost but the purchase price as a justification for ignoring operating costs. Rowley,[1] for example, discusses the costs of online searching and suggests that an inability to estimate the costs of online services in advance may be a problem for library managers who are used to predicting costs for tangibles. It is true that purchase prices are the most easily identifiable costs, but if you have an adequate framework for examining all of the costs associated with a system, the task of cost estimation becomes significantly easier. The estimates may be less accurate to begin with, but as Chapter 1 suggests, even inaccurate estimates are better than none.

Estimates of costs can always be modified if they later prove to be inaccurate, while the act of formulating estimates forces the manager to consider, at least, what areas might create costs. Crowe and Light describe a case which shows how a consortium involved all of its staff in a participative procurement exercise.[2] The Peninsula Library System – a consortium of eight libraries in the San Mateo area of California – wished to estimate the costs of future shared automation efforts, and, rather than hire a consultant, approached three vendors directly: 'We needed to know if we could afford what our staff clearly thought was the best system and how that vendor compared to others in terms of pricing.'

Crowe and Light point out that first impressions can be misleading: on the basis of the figures provided by the three competing vendors, the product most desired by staff appeared to be the most expensive. But after the team had negotiated a discount, and asked the vendor to consider a different hardware platform, the quote on the final configuration for the preferred option was similar to the others proposed by the vendors and was thus more affordable.

Involvement of all participative staff in the costing process had spin-off benefits: 'We began to examine new ways to implement and administer our automation operation, with staff involvement again being crucial. The project has allowed us to redesign our operations to provide improved technology services with lower operating costs to the member libraries and users'.

HOW TO LOOK FOR COSTS USING LIFE-CYCLE COSTING

One method of better estimating costs is adapted from a decision-making technique known as **life-cycle costing**. Readers should be aware that the concepts of costing discussed below are only a part of life cycle costing (LCC), a decision-making technique for investment. A more comprehensive discussion of LCC is presented in Chapter 4.

Life-cycle costing (LCC) is a decision-making technique that attempts to take into account all of an asset's costs during the lifetime of that asset. There is no set formula for incorporating all of an asset's costs in an estimate, so it may be more useful to think of LCC as framework for examining the cost of assets that points us to areas where we may incur costs. To do this, LCC identifies three major cost areas:

1   development and decision costs;
2   purchase and installation costs; and
3   annual operating costs.

Development and decision costs

These are costs which are associated with deciding if and what kinds of assets should be acquired. Depending on the type of asset or system, the costs of simply trying to decide what to purchase may be very large. A classic case of this occurs in building projects. Large fees are often necessary to pay architects, surveyors, attorneys and accountants and other consultants to devise a plan to build before a single shovel of dirt is moved or a brick is laid. Similar expenses may be incurred in systems analysis projects for large automation systems.

Some organizations do not regard the time spent by their employees in making acquisition decisions as a cost, reasoning that their employees are already paid for, so they should not be considered as an expense. This may be true to the extent that they require no additional funding, but it is important to remember that employee time is a finite resource. Time spent making decisions is time that cannot be used for some other organizational task, and it is therefore appropriate to include the cost of an employee's time as part of the development cost for purchasing an asset.

Purchase and installation costs

Purchase costs are frequently the only costs that organizations take into account and should be self-explanatory. However, many other costs are associated with acquiring and making an asset operational and should be taken into account. The following list of cost categories is not meant to be exhaustive, but it is a general list of costs usually associated with the purchase of most electronic system assets.

Removal of old assets

This is often a small expense, but depending on the nature of the old asset, it may be significant: physical removal of an old asset may be expensive. A large asset may have been installed prior to the completion of a room, in which case partial demolition may be needed in order to remove it. In another case, the old asset may be toxic. An old transformer may contain PCBs for example, in which case disposal becomes expensive and difficult.

Freight and delivery

Very large assets may need special handling and the services of a heavy truck or crane, for example. If delivery is to be from a distant location, substantial shipping or transport costs may be necessary.

Bringing large assets into a new setting can also present installation problems similar to those of removing old assets in that structural modifications may be needed before new equipment can be installed.

Installation

Depending on the asset, the cost of pre-installation preparation of the site may be significant. This seems to be particularly common in the case of automated systems. Computers, for example, may need uninterruptable power sources, communications cabling, or special cooling and ventilation systems. It is not unusual to watch an automation system being off-loaded into a work-site, only to have its new owners discover that they have too few electrical outlets for the equipment or that the system regularly crashes because the room in which it was installed overheats.

Computers may also change work environments which may need to be further modified in order to accommodate the needs of their operators. Organizations frequently place facilities such as computer lab clusters in isolated rooms without windows since computers are usually easier to operate out of direct sunlight. Planners may forget, however, that the introduction of extra staff to what might have formerly been a storeroom may overtax the room's ventilation system. Expensive modifications may then be necessary before the room can be used comfortably.

The tendency for companies to place computers in storerooms sometimes exposes environmental hazards and it is not unusual for work-crews to uncover asbestos or similar hazards which require. expensive removal before the site can be used.

Finally, many sites will require expensive modifications such as ramps or widened doorways if it is necessary to make them accessible for the disabled. More than one public computing site has been forced to dismantle and move because it could not comply with legal requirements that it should be made accessible to the disabled.

Training

What needs to be done to insure that the organization's employees are competent to use a system? The time and effort needed to become proficient in some systems is frequently a major cost. There may be direct expenses such as sending employees on courses, but managers also need to consider the cost of productivity losses that occur while employees learn how to use the new system and of the loss of other activities that can't take place while staff train. Many organizations ignore training costs because the employees are 'already paid for'. But these losses are a cost and they should be accounted for as such.

Annual operating costs

These are the expenses incurred in the daily operation of the asset. Organizations usually acquire assets or systems for use over a number of years. Viewed over the total lifetime of a system, total operating costs can be very high.

Annual operating costs are largely built-in at the point at which the organization acquires the asset. That is, once a system is operating, there is very little control that can be exercised over its operating costs apart from reducing the level of service provided. In the case of fax machines cited above, the organization is forced to use thermal paper if it has purchased a fax machine that won't run on ordinary paper. They may opt to receive fewer faxes or find a cheaper vendor, but they have little control over the cost of receiving faxes.

Control over operating expenses is largely exercised at the decision and development stages of acquiring assets. As a general rule, the greater the effort expended at the development stage, the lower the operating costs will be.

Materials

What special materials are required to keep the system running? Direct materials such as printer paper and toner cartridges for printers are obvious operating costs. Managers also need to be sensitive to the costs of finding appropriate materials. For example, it is known that at least one library with which the authors have dealt made a special 'bargain' purchase of off-brand printers. The printers worked adequately for the first few months until the time came for their ribbons to be replaced. The local office supply store did not stock ribbons for the library's printers and it was only after a week's investigation that a supplier was found. In the end, the director decided that the cost of finding replacement parts and the ill-will generated by the poorly operating printers was greater than the costs of purchasing new printers would have been.

Software

Does the system need special software before it will run and does that software need to be upgraded at regular intervals? Many systems are updated at regular intervals and additional software modifications must be made in order to continue running the system. In many cases these updates will be included as part of the purchase price, but this practice is by no means universal.

An even greater problem may occur in cases where the organization has opted for custom-designed software. An evaluation of the criteria for making the decision between commercial and custom-designed software is beyond the scope of this book and more properly dealt with as part of the systems analysis process. There are, however, several financial issues that managers need to keep in mind concerning software.

1 Updating custom software is almost invariably more expensive than modifying commercial software. Custom programming is usually more time-consuming and expensive than installing a supplier-generated update.
2 The likelihood of system problems occurring is usually higher in custom software, while problems are usually more difficult and expensive to diagnose and repair in it. The original creators may have gone out of business or failed to document their work adequately and their system may have to be abandoned.

This is not to say that custom software does not make economic sense in some cases, only that its operating costs may be greater than that of an off-the-shelf purchase. The potential gain in productivity the software offers should be examined in the light of what may be its higher operating costs. Once you have installed a system, regardless of whether it is commercial or custom-designed, you are committed to it and will have little control over its operating cost.

Utilities

How much power does the system require? This should include not only the direct utility usage by the system, but also any climate control costs. Some systems are significantly more sensitive to their environments than others and require significant moisture and temperature control. Similarly, computer terminals produce a significant heat output which can render rooms in which they are installed uninhabitable. Ventilation and air conditioning costs may be more substantial than the direct utility costs of running the computer and no less necessary.

Labor

How many people are needed to operate the system? Do they need to acquire special skills (expensively) and are those skills available within the organization? Some systems may carry lower price tags but be more difficult to learn or operate. A good example of this can be found in the point of sale (POS) systems used in fast-food restaurants. These systems list many of the items for sale on the cash till's key pads as items rather than simply as numbers and can therefore be used by employees with very little training. The reason for this is the high turnover among fast-food employees: there is little time to train an employee and the increased productivity achieved justifies the use of a more expensive but more easily learned system.

Maintenance

How often does the asset break down and what is the cost of repairing it? Seemingly inexpensive assets may carry substantial repair costs as part of their normal operating cost. Many of us have had the experience of buying an inexpensive automobile that cost more in repair bills than the price difference for a more expensive but more reliable brand. A similar problem can arise in the case of assets that have substantial repair costs.

COMBINING COST INFORMATION

An important consideration when you are gathering system cost information from a variety of sources is to be sure that all of your costs are converted to a common activity base, otherwise you won't be comparing like with like.

WORKED EXAMPLE: LEASING

You have decided to lease a copy machine for which you have gathered the following cost information:

	$
Estimated copies per month	2,000
Estimated hours of operation per month	80
Lease cost/month	200
Maintenance/year	5,000
Electricity/operating hour	1.50
Toner cartridges (each: 1 cartridge is good for 3000 copies)	85

How much will the copier cost to run for one year?

	$
Lease cost/year	
12 × 200	2,400
Electricity/year	
80 × 12 × 1.50	1,440
Toner/year	
2000 × 12/3000 × 85	680
Maintenance/year	500
Total	5,020

The costs in this case have all been converted to a yearly basis, but there is no reason why they couldn't have been calculated monthly, hourly, or on a per-copy basis depending on the needs of management.

WORKED EXAMPLE: DETERMINING THE COSTS FOR AN INTERNET CONNECTION

Our discussions up to this point have largely been hypothetical but we will now attempt to apply our cost categories to a real automation system. For the purposes of illustration, we will use the example of establishing an Internet connection for a department within a larger academic organization. In order to do this, we will make the following assumptions about the volume of users:

Level 1:

Total user population:	450
Number of simultaneous users at a given time	40

Level 2:

Total user population:	1,000
Number of simultaneous users at a given time	180

Level 3:

Total user population:	1,500
Number of simultaneous users at a given time	230

Our department will purchase its own hardware and software, but the day-to-day maintenance will be undertaken by a contractual agreement with the university's computing services.

The following list of equipment and services is needed to provided this level of service.

		$
1	SPARC Server (including tape backup and 4 gigabytes of memory: maximum capacity 1200 users)	15,000
2	Machine room space rental/year (yearly rental in the university computing service, this reflects the space taken up by one SPARC server	300
3	Terminal server (to manage up to 120 modems)	2,000
4	Modems	
	1 modem/simultaneous user*	
	Rack-mounted	500
	Stand-alone	250

*The user has a choice of stand-alone or rack-mounted modems. The purchase price of a rack-mounted modem is twice that of a stand-alone. The maintenance costs are substantially lower, however.

		$
5	T-I connection to the Internet backbone	

(A T-I is the connection to the Internet source provider:
maximum capacity 1200 users)

This component has two parts:

		$
Installation fee (one-time fee for each T-I connection)		4,000
Usage charge/month (monthly fee for the use of the T-I connection)		1,000
6	Router CSU/DSU (one router per T-I connection)	2,500
7	Local phone connections	

Installation fee (one-time fee for connection by local phone
service provider: maximum line capacity of 200 simultaneous
users/line)   1,000

Monthly phone usage charge (flat fee for up to 200
simultaneous users)   400

In addition to the hardware costs, it is estimated that six hours of an attorney's time will be required to write contracts. The attorney bills at the rate of $70 per hour. We can therefore summarize comparative costs as follows:

	40 users $	180 users $	230 users $
1 Development and decision costs			
Attorney Fees	420	420	420
2 Purchase and installation costs			
SPARC server	15,000	15,000	30,000
Terminal server	2,000	4,000	6,000
Modems	20,000	90,000	115,000
T-I installation	4,000	4,000	8,000
Router	2,500	2,500	5,000
Phone installation	1,000	1,000	2,000
	44,920	116,920	166,420
3 Yearly operating costs			
Machine space rental	300	300	600
T-I use	12,000	12,000	24,000
Phone line	4,800	4,800	9,600
	17,100	17,100	34,200

Note that it was necessary to convert the monthly costs of the phone line and T-I use to yearly amounts in order to combine them with the machine space rental which is charged yearly. The conversion was trivial in this case, but it is important to keep in mind that all of the system's costs need to have the same activity base.

A comparison of the three service levels reveals several important aspects of the system's cost.

1 The start-up costs for the system are very high. For most electronic services, extensive installation and maintenance have to be added to purchase costs.

2 Nearly all of the costs for the Internet system are fixed, regardless of the level of service. Those costs which appear to vary actually do so only on a yearly basis, but not according to changes in the volume of users. Thus, within the capacity of the system, the number of users can vary to a relatively large degree without an affect on system operating costs.

3 Understanding where the relevant ranges occur for the fixed costs becomes vital in costing out systems for different levels of service. Fixed costs remain unchanged for relatively wide fluctuations in activity, but can be very high when they do increase. Thus, the operating costs are identical for Levels 1 and 2, but the number of simultaneous users at Level 2 is more than four times that at Level 1. In contrast, the increase in simultaneous users between Level 2 and Level 3 is less than 30% but the operating costs double.

ANALYZING COSTS FOR THE LIFE OF THE SYSTEM

We have noted earlier that yearly operating costs can be substantial in the context of the entire life of the system. In our Internet example, we have more than one year of operating costs to take into consideration. Costs that occur in future years, however, require more than a simple additive treatment since the value of money changes over time. Readers are advised that other techniques will be needed to better understand aspects of costing the system and that these will be covered in subsequent sections of this book, notably Chapter 4.

SUMMARY OF BASIC COSTING PROCEDURES

Basic costing procedures may be summarized as follows.

1   Gather all of the relevant cost components of the system. This requires attention to how the system operates. Gathering information is the cornerstone of any costing system: the cost estimates will only be as good as the system information that generates them.

2   Categorize each item in the list of cost components according to the way in which the cost varies with different levels of activity. For each cost you will also have to make the following decisions:

    (a) What activity base is most useful for the managerial decisions I need to make? (Be sure that all of the costs are prepared on the same basis.)

    (b) What is the relevant range for the costs? Do the rates for variable costs change? Where and how? At what level of activity do the fixed costs increase/decrease?

3   Combine the total system costs for various projected levels of service.

After completing these steps, you should have a comprehensive list of all of the costs associated with an automated system. This is probably the single most important step that you as a manager can take to manage the finances of a system you plan to install.

It still remains to combine and analyze these costs to make the decisions concerning investments, pricing and managerial control that form the basis for the remainder of the book. However, the foundation for any analysis must always be the original cost data. None of the manager's analyses, or the subsequent decisions that result from them are of any value without accurate cost data.

We conclude this chapter with some exercises designed to help you to develop skills in classifying and allocating costs.

EXERCISE ONE: EXTERNAL CLIENTS

Background

Your library has decided to offer a service to local businesses in which they phone or e-mail questions to the library which delivers written responses. The following costs are associated with the program.

1 The Director devotes 10% of her time to the project each month, her yearly salary is $45000.
2 A library secretary spends eight hours each week typing invoices for the program. She is paid $1100 a month.
3 A librarian works one-half time on the project. He is paid $28,000 a year.
4 The program has purchased a new fax machine for $600 with an estimated life of three years. Each request from a business requires an average of three faxes to administer. The cost of producing a fax is $1.
5 The library has purchased a computer for conducting searches at a cost of $4000 and it has an expected life of three years.
6 The following costs are associated with the library facility:

   (a) mortgage: $1900/month;
   (b) utilities: $1100/month;
   (c) umbrella insurance policies: $4000/year; and
   (d) assessments from regional library consortium: $500/quarter.

Questions
1 Based on the information presented above, what are the total costs associated with the service? Base your decisions on the best estimates you have of how the organization is likely to operate.
2 Which costs are fixed and which are variable?
3 Which costs provide future value, i.e. which are assets?

Sample answers
1 Directors salary: $45,000/year (fixed). The cost is allocated based on the Director's estimate of her worktime devoted to the service ($45,000 × 10%). The expense is probably best categorized as fixed since there is no clear connection between the level of activity (e.g. the number of calls) and the amount of time she spends on the project. However, since the Director has determined that the 10% of his/her time is devoted specifically to the program, this expense should be categorized as a direct overhead. The best evidence for this is that the Director is salaried and it is therefore unlikely that her salary (and by extension the amount of it allocated to the program) will not change during the course of the year, based on the level of the program's activity.
2 Secretary's salary: $2640 (fixed). The cost is calculated on the basis of 20% (8/40) of the secretary's annual commitment to the project (1100 × 0.2 × 12 = 2640). The rationale for categorizing this as a fixed cost

is similar to that for the Director's salary: a proportion of the secretary's time is known to be related specifically to the program, but there is no clear indication that it varies directly with any known level of activity.

3   Librarian's salary. $14,000 (fixed). In this case the total time devoted to the program is specified. Since the librarian is described as salaried, we assume that the amount he or she is to be paid will not change during the year.

4   Fax costs: the $600 purchase price for the fax machine represents the exchange of one asset for another of equal value. Since we expect benefit over a period of three years, we would reduce the book value of the fax machine over this period. This cost is likely to be fixed since it does not vary with a level of activity. Note that the outflow of cash occurs only in the year of purchase and that the subsequent depreciation of the fax machine does not affect cash flow. Each individual request also carries a variable cost of $3.00 (3 faxes @ $1.00 each) since this cost varies directly with the number of requests made.

5   Computer: $4000 (fixed). The cost results in cash leaving the organization, but only in exchange for an equally valued asset.

6   The yearly costs of the mortgage, utilities, insurance and assessments from the regional consortium total $42,000 for the entire library. The library manager would need to decide if and how to allocate part of this to the program. One rationale might be that outside users need to pay for a portion of the library overhead since they could not receive the service without these expenses being incurred. A contrary position might be that the library pays the expenses anyway and that as a matter of public service, businesses would be assessed only for those costs directly associated with the program.

Assuming that a decision is made to allocate part of the library overhead to the program, some basis for allocation will be necessary. The example does not provide sufficient information to determine a basis, but possible methods might include an assessment based on the floor space taken up by the program, since most of the overhead is related to the physical premises, or alternatively the number of labor hours devoted to the service.

EXERCISE TWO: IN-HOUSE PRODUCTS

Background

You are the Director of a library and your library has decided to produce its own educational videos. The manager proposes two levels of production: Level 1 (60 videos/year) and Level 2 (110 videos/year). The equipment needed to produce the videos has the following system costs (assume a useful life of four years for the assets).

1 Purchase price: $15,000 (the equipment can produce 95 videos/year).
2 Software to operate the equipment: $3500.
3 Yearly software upgrades: $800.
4 Because of the vast array of systems available, you estimate it will take you 30 hours of research and consulting with vendors to choose one of them. Your annual salary is $29,000 (assume a 2000-hour work year).
5 The new system requires a darkened work area and a new power source. The fees for providing these are $1600 and $900 respectively.
6 It is estimated that maintenance of the equipment will cost $890 per year.
7 The unit will consume an additional $560 in electrical power each year.
8 Approximately $1800 will be spent annually on materials.

Question
What are the total costs for the system for both levels of service?

Sample answer

	Service Level 1 $	Service Level 2 $
Development costs:		
Director's salary	435	435
Purchase and installation costs:		
Work area	1,600	1,600
Power source	900	900
Purchase price	15,000	30,000
Software	3,500	7,000
Yearly operating costs:		
Software upgrades	800	1,600
Maintenance	890	1,780
Electrical power	560	1,020
Materials	1,800	3,290

It was assumed in this case that it would be necessary to purchase double the amount of production equipment and software for the higher level of service. The installation costs were doubled for the purposes of simplifying the example, but it is also possible that some of the installation work would accommodate a second machine. Both the electrical power and materials are likely to be variable and have been calculated on a pro rata basis on the number of videos produced. As we have noted earlier, the numbers in the example represent only the beginning of the costing process. The total variable costs need to be examined for the entire life of the system.

EXERCISE THREE: RUNNING COSTS

Background
The following is a list of costs associated with running a library:

	$
Director's salary/year	40,000
Fax copies/month (50 faxes)	30
Fax machine payments/month	55
Copier paper/month (4000 copies)	250
Copier lease payments/month	900
Clerk's pay/hour	6
Insurance/year	1,200
Mortgage/month	1,900
Air conditioner depreciation/month	200
Utilities/month	500

Question
Decide whether each cost is fixed or variable, giving reasons.

Sample answer
The starting point for system managers attempting a cost analysis is to examine how each of the costs changes with levels of activities in the organization. The key to determining if a cost is fixed or variable is to look at its behavior in terms of local managerial control rather than to decide on the basis of a general belief of how similarly labeled costs behave in other organizational settings. That is, a given cost may be fixed for a particular manager even if we generally think of the cost as variable (note, for example, the costs for utilities and clerk's wages below).

1   Director's salary: $40,000 (fixed). In all likelihood the director is paid on a yearly contract basis and his or her salary is unlikely to change regardless of the number of hours the director works.
2   Fax copies: $30 (variable). The average cost of a single fax is $0.60.
3   Fax and copier lease payments: $55, $900 (fixed). Generally, leases do not fall below a set amount even if the organization does not use the

machine. In some cases, though, an additional fee is payable if the organizational usage rises above a predetermined maximum level, making it a mixed cost. For example, the terms of the copier lease might read $900/month plus $0.02 per copy for any copies in excess of 4000. If the number of copies produced was 6000, the copier costs would be $940 (2000 × 0.02 = $40). The $40 is variable, but the $900 base payment is fixed.

4   Copier paper: $250 (variable). The number of sheets of paper used will almost certainly vary with the number of copies made. In this case, the average cost of a sheet of copy paper is $0.0625.

5   Clerk's pay: $6 (variable). If the clerk is paid on an hourly basis, the amount of hourly pay will vary in accordance with the number of hours he or she works. Managers should be careful, however, to determine that the clerk's pay really does vary. Many workers are only listed in organizational records as being paid on an hourly basis because they are eligible to receive overtime rates. Civil service or union regulations may specify that they are guaranteed a minimum number of hours each week. In such cases, the base salary is a fixed expense and any overtime rate (which usually is paid in hourly increments) is a variable cost.

6   Insurance, mortgage, air conditioner depreciation: $1200, $1900, $200 (fixed). These costs generally do not vary with levels of activities. Remember from Chapter 1 that a depreciation cost does not represent a flow of cash out of the organization.

7   Utilities: $500 (fixed or variable depending on the context). Utilities such as heat and electricity are variable to the extent that they change in relationship to conditions such as the number of hours lights are left on or the temperature at which a building is kept. From a manager's perspective, though, most of these costs are likely to be fixed. In most cases, power consumption for maintaining minimal climate control levels and safety features such as outside lighting or security systems cannot be significantly reduced.

REFERENCES

1   Rowley, J., 'How much will my online search cost? A review of the charging policies of the online hosts', *Online and CD ROM review*, **17** (3), June 1993, 143–8.

2   Crowe, L. and Light, J., 'Desperately seeking a system', *Library journal*, **119** (16), 1994, October 1, 42–4.

CHAPTER 3

Allocating costs

Imagine the following scene in the break room as Arthur Trent, Assistant Head of Technical Services at Mega Library, sits down with his fellow librarians.

SCENARIO

'Angels and ministers of grace defend us from so-called experts who've read only one book,' Arthur muttered.

'Arthur, what seems to be the trouble?' said a colleague.

'It's the new Director,' he replied. 'He's just come back from a seminar in responsibility-centered management, and he's decided that each department will now be individually responsible for a part of the University's overhead. I am now being evaluated on how well I am able to cover such expenses as campus security and research and development. As if anything I did or could do would change those figures.'

'Sounds a bit unfair,' said a second colleague.

'Unfair. It's positively absurd,' said Arthur. 'I haven't told you the silliest bits yet. He's decided that all these expenses will be shared according to the floor space that we're occupying. I suppose I could live with that for maintenance or the light bill, but R and D? I think I've out maneuvered him on that one though: I've shoved all the desks together and reduced our floor space by 20%. The clerks are complaining about being cramped, but what am I supposed to do? I can't very well ask campus security to make do with cars that won't start.'

'Can't be very good for productivity, being all crammed together,' said another member of the lunch group.

'It gets worse,' said Arthur. 'The Director has also decided that each worker at a terminal will now be evaluated on the basis of the expenses that terminal incurs. As if a clerk had any discretion

about that. They're all sick with worry that they won't get a raise if their figures are too high. They're all running around the library turning off lights and counting paper clips instead of inputting records. Two of my best people have already put in for transfers to the Bursar's office where it's less crazy. Frankly, I can't blame them, I'd leave myself if could find another job. Do you suppose it's too late to learn poultry farming?'

COSTS IN CONTEXT

The above scenario has been exaggerated for the purposes of illustration, but it represents what can happen when the zeal for spreading the responsibility for costs goes beyond the bounds of what may be regarded as sensible. We referred in the last chapter to the need for allocating indirect costs properly so that decisions about, for example, adding new services, evaluating managerial performance, encouraging or discouraging the use of organizational resources such as computers or maintenance and setting prices or justifying costs, can be made on a more rational basis. In this chapter, we look at cost allocation in more detail.

As we see from the scenario, costs need to be allocated on a basis other than a simple algorithmic application of costs to activities. This is not to say that accurate cost gathering and application are not crucial to understanding the costs of application, but there are managerial considerations which mean that a more sophisticated approach is needed. In this chapter we will begin by exploring the techniques of cost allocation, and then go on to examine how and when to assign costs to help organizational goals and employee performance.

WHY ALLOCATE COSTS?

There are two basic outcomes from allocating costs: better economic decisions and better motivation. As regards the first, management seeks to better understand the 'true' cost of a particular product or service. The outcome of better economic knowledge should be better decision-making or better pricing of services provided against

may be some value in knowing the costs associated with an individual workstation (the issue which was particularly demoralizing in our scenario) but it seems more productive to assume that individual costing responsibility is better exercised at a higher level in the organization. Data entry clerks cannot regulate the amount of internal business they do in the library, so it makes little sense to treat them as individual entrepreneurs.

A similar example might be found in a library with a number of decentralized branches, each of which has separate departments such as technical services, automation, reference, etc. Since each library (and their individual departments) are managed separately, looking at technical services as a cost center across multiple branches would be of limited use.

Another example is a reference service distributed across institutions sharing a common technical platform, where expertise is pooled and a service is delivered on a rota basis across a network. Let's say, in the first instance, that the five participating institutions agree that the project is to be managed on a consortium basis. In this case it makes sense to treat the service as a cost objective which will be shared by the participants. In an alternative scenario, however, whereby the five institutions agree to a more loosely participative arrangement, it may make more sense to treat each institution's individual reference service as a cost objective.

These examples make this principle of usefulness look obvious, but a large number of organizations collect financial information in ways that are not useful to managers, simply because the information has always been collected that way. Inertia and tradition can exert strong forces in record keeping and managers should not assume that a library's financial records are necessarily useful. Reorganizations, mergers and workflow changes due to increased automation may create significant changes in the organization that are not mirrored by changes in the financial records.

Conversely, managers need to be aware of the cost associated with changing and maintaining record systems. In some cases, the costs of reorganization outweigh any benefits that more responsive records might offer. Managers need to be aware of the cost of finding the costs, a consideration that should be included (ideally) in any plan for organizational restructuring.

A second consideration in choosing cost centers is controllability. A trend in many organizations is to decentralize, to push decision-making into lower levels of the organization. The risk in decentralization is that of pushing responsibility for costs into levels of the organization where the managers have no effective control over them. Generally, the lower one proceeds in an organization, the fewer the costs that are controllable. It makes little sense to force managers to be accountable for costs over which they have no discretion. Evaluation based on factors that are outside an employee's control reduces morale and is less useful for assessing performance, as in the case of our clerks leaving for other departments.

Poor cost allocation can also force managers to make absurd decisions that cut their individual costs without changing the overall expenses of the organization. In the earlier scenario, we saw that the department manager was forced to make his employees work less efficiently in order to cut costs.

POOLING COSTS

Why pool costs?

It is theoretically possible to assign costs separately to individual activities but in most cases the effort and cost involved in achieving this level of analysis is prohibitive. Moreover, in many cases such analysis may not be operationally possible. Administrative costs, for example, may not be directly traceable in their entirety to any specific department or service. Instead, we can combine costs according to a variety of associative schemes such as their application to departments and allocate the resulting aggregate costs in order to arrive at better costing decisions.

Approaches to pooling costs

Costs can be pooled (i.e. grouped or aggregated) in a variety of ways including whether they are fixed or variable and/or according to their degree of homogeneity or how similar they are in their causal relationship with the relevant cost objective. Some of the most common methods of pooling costs are those which relate to departments and to products. Both approaches to pooling are now discussed in greater detail.

Departmental cost pooling

Costs are often assigned to particular units or subunits (i.e. departments) in an organization.

WORKED EXAMPLE: COSTING A UNIT OF REFERENCE SERVICE

For example, assume that a reference department has the following costs for one year of operation:

	$
Direct labor costs	50,000
Librarian salaries	
Clerical salaries for	
reference clerks	
Direct materials costs	40,000
Connect time	
Licensing fees	
Reference materials	
Indirect departmental costs	30,000
Reference equipment depreciation	
Reference administration salaries	
Allocated overhead costs	20,000
Costs transferred from other depts.	
Total reference department costs	140,000

In the departmental costing approach, all of the relevant costs are first combined to arrive at the total costs for the department. The cost of providing a unit of service (in this case a reference transaction) is then determined by distributing the total costs of the department amongst each unit of service. If the reference department carries out 10,000 reference requests each year, then the departmental cost of a transaction is $14 ($140,000 ÷ 10,000).

Product/service cost pooling

Departmental costing has the advantage of simplicity, but it is criticized as a technique because it focuses on the department rather than the service or product of an organization. Not all services within a department need the same level of resource input. This distinction is important because, in most libraries, understanding the costs of different services is crucial to understanding the financial impact of providing those services to various groups of users.

WORKED EXAMPLE: TWO-TIER SERVICE

Imagine that our reference department actually deals with two classes of user. One is made up of standard public reference users and the other of commercial users who need business and investment data. The latter service requires a significantly higher resource input in terms of both labor and connect time. The costs for each service are as follows:

	Public user transaction $	Commercial user transaction $	Average cost $
Direct labor costs	1.00	4.00	5.00
Direct materials costs	1.00	3.00	4.00
Other indirect costs	5.00	5.00	5.00
Total costs	7.00	12.00	14.00

In most industries, it would be foolish to assume that all products cost similar amounts to produce, so it should come as no surprise that library services, a sector where product customization can be very important, have varying costs for different classes of users. How important is this to library operations? The answer depends on what decision is being made and on the nature of the library user concerned. Assigning costs on a departmental level is probably sufficient for running the department itself, if the user population is largely homogeneous (an assumption that misguidedly seems to underlay costing practice in some libraries) or if there is no need to add to or reduce services. If, however, a decision concerning levels of service and/or the pricing of services has to be made, product/service costing will provide more accurate information, and, by extension, a better decision.

Librarians are, however, often reluctant to classify costs by user group. It is difficult to reconcile this method with the prevailing ethos of providing a universal service to diverse user groups, and many librarians prefer to operate on the basis of an assumed norm, rather than empirical measures of user need. In the latter case, the cost of obtaining the costs may outweigh the potential benefit of greater managerial control; it may be difficult to collect cost information, especially if it involves users' perceptions of costs.[1] Here, the dictates of costs vs. benefits of collecting better cost information should obtain. Insofar as the ethos of universal public service free at point of use is concerned, however, librarians should be aware that libraries, in common with most other organizations, do not have unlimited resources. Services are ultimately limited by availability of funds, if for no other reason. It is usually better to control where and when services will be limited rather than having chance dictate where the money will run out.

COST ALLOCATION

What costs should be allocated?

What costs really need to be collected and allocated to a cost center to help managers understand and control costs? The simplest approach is to take all of the organizational costs and allocate them on some basis to each department. The difficulty with this approach is that a direct cause and effect relationship between costs and the activities that generate them reaches only so far in an organization. At some point, usually very quickly, there is no discernible relationship between changes in the cost center's activity and changes in the organizational level of indirect costs. Often, the decisions to make large investments in fixed assets or organizational overhead such as administration or research and development occur at high levels of the organization with very little connection between departmental operations.

The converse, however, is that while the decision to offer various services may not immediately produce a change in the general organizational overhead, the cumulative effects of offering the services result in increasing costs overall within the organization. In most organizations, particularly those with high-cost assets such as computers, there can be gradual 'creep' upward of costs from lower organizational units to the organization as a whole.

The allocation of at least some fixed and indirect costs helps offset the inevitable increases in such costs that occur in all organizations. The criterion of cause and effect should be the starting point for allocation; however, since completely accurate cost usage information is often costly, if not impossible to obtain, some easy substitute is necessary that approximates usage by various subunits of the organization. At a minimum, some flat fee, regardless of the level of usage by the department, may be desirable simply to let managers know that such costs exist.

Allocation bases

In theory, allocated expenses may have many cost pools and many bases. (We will go into this in more detail in a subsequent section of this chapter which concerns activity-based costing where you will find an extended discussion of multiple bases and cost pools.) In practice, however, it is desirable to have fewer cost bases and pools rather than more, on the assumption that one variable, such as direct labor dollars, can act as predictor (to a reasonable degree) all similar overhead costs. As we have discussed, the ideal for a cost-activity basis is causal, but it is often difficult to establish one. More often, allocation is made on a co-variant basis (i.e. where cost usages follow the same trends) with overhead even if there is no direct causal linkage.

The selection of cost allocation bases is usually made after consideration of the following criteria:

1   How clearly does the basis connect the cost of services in the pool with the benefits that result from the services? The strongest relationship is causal, but we normally settle for an

associative basis (one that varies similarly with levels of activity even if there is no causal relationship).

2   What are the costs of gathering and analyzing information for use with the basis? Bases that are too complicated run the risk of costing more to implement than the value of the improved decision-making that they may provide.

3   How material is the difference among bases? If there is little difference between the choices for cost allocation it is normally more cost-effective to choose the cheapest.

Overall, cost allocation bases should be as simple and easy to apply as possible. Managers to whom the costs are to be applied, should, in particular, be able to follow how and why those costs originated.

Common allocation bases

Any number of bases could be used for allocating costs depending on the nature of the activity. Subsequent sections of this chapter will deal with activity-based costing, but the following is a general description and critique of the most common and simple methods of allocating costs.

Direct labor hours

Labor hours are the classic basis for allocation in a manufacturing environment in which labor provides the greatest amount of added value to the final product. Labor may also be appropriate for service industries in which the greatest portion of expense for the service is labor (e.g. original manuscript cataloging that does not require an automated service.) The use of labor hours as a basis for cost measurement in such circumstances often provides the best indication of other expenses. Many costs such as depreciation and interest are directly related to time. Similarly, many administrative overhead costs such as payroll are also directly related to the elapsed time of work.

A major criticism of using direct labor hours as a basis is that labor plays an increasingly small role in many operations. This is particularly true in an electronic information services environment, for example, where much of the labor is performed via automation with little actual human labor (such as batch processing payroll records) or in which the automated equipment is so expensive that its cost is far greater than the cost of the labor needed to run it. The labor cost of maintaining circulation records, for example, is small compared to the cost of buying and running the integrated library system of which circulation is but a part.

Direct labor dollars

In cases where labor rates are uniform, there are no material differences between using labor dollars and labor hours as an allocation basis. In such cases, it is usually better to use hours, since elapsed work time has a more logical connection with overhead than dollars (see above). Labor dollars makes sense as a basis in cases where higher salaried workers are responsible for a greater proportion of the resources used in production or service.

Machine hours

In highly mechanized or automated electronic processes, machine time may be a better predictor of overhead use than labor. Depreciation, access fees and licensing fees are all heavily dependent on machine use and usually vary directly in accordance with it. A drawback to the use of machine time may be the difficulty of gathering cost data. Some systems are not able to monitor how long and for what purpose they are used. But integrated library management systems or online connect systems usually have features that provide such information. In cases where machine time cannot be accounted for separately, labor hours can sometimes be used if they co-vary; that is, if no machine operates without an employee. More frequently in library settings, labor hours may be less useful since many systems are now designed to be operated by users without the aid of an intermediary.

ACTIVITY-BASED COSTING

The increased use of automation and computerized services has led to a decline in the importance of labor as a primary cost in producing services. As a result, relying on direct labor hours (or any simple allocation basis) as the primary cost allocation basis can produce large distortions in the allocation of overhead costs. The need for more accurate costing for products and services has therefore led to the widespread adoption of activity-based costing (ABC) instead. In this section we will examine what ABC is, the advantages of using it to cost services and demonstrate how to apply ABC in a library automation setting. Readers needing more detail are referred to Cooper.[2]

ABC defined

Activity-based costing attempts to assign overhead based on the activities that cause overhead costs to be incurred, rather than arbitrarily assigning costs simply because the organization incurs them. Traditionally, overhead has been treated as having little or no causal relationship with levels of service. Activity-based costing, however, operates on the premise that many of the costs that are treated as overhead are, in fact, variable costs. Examining overhead costs can uncover cause and effect relationships that link activities with overhead costs.

For example, few libraries would view computer maintenance as a direct cost, with the result that the costs of the maintenance department are usually allocated according to a simple algorithmic basis such as the number of work orders. However, what if the high-end graphics work-stations used in the library media work were significantly more complex and thus more time-consuming and expensive to maintain? Using the number of work orders as a basis would distort the amount of repair work used to support the media lab.

Activity-based costing deals with this allocation problem by examining the activities performed by computer maintenance and establishing a set of **cost drivers**. That is, by identifying the activity that causes or drives the consumption of costs. In the earlier example, machine type would be a more accurate predictor of repair costs than simple allocation.

Why use ABC?

The primary benefit of using ABC is more accurate costing. Advocates of ABC contend that most organizations have a poor idea of the actual costs of providing products or services they offer. In most organizations, direct labor has declined as a major input for production and the volume of indirect costs has grown. Product and service costs based on a simple allocation basis are already distorted. Further, the distortions caused by simple allocation bases will produce even greater distortions as increasing computerization reduces the level of direct labor. Any organization that relies on such inaccurate cost information will evaluate the use of its resources incorrectly and inevitably make poor investment and pricing decisions.

A related benefit of better costing is likely to be better managerial decisions. As managers become aware of the true costs of their departments and their consumption of services, they can make choices that make better use of limited organizational resources. In the earlier example, the media lab's computer maintenance was being subsidized by the rest of the library under a simple allocation system. Under an activity-based system that passes the true costs of maintenance to the media lab, there will probably be a decline in the number of non-essential maintenance requests.

Implementing activity-based costing

Allocating costs in an ABC system is no different, in principle, than any allocation process. The steps involved are:

1 select the products/services for which costs are to be gathered;
2 assign the direct costs;
3 examine each overhead cost associated with the product/service to determine if some cost driver exists that predicts (either causes or at least co-varies with) the overhead cost; and
4 apply any remaining overhead using a standard basis.

Activity-based costing differs from traditional costing to the extent that it relies on multiple activity-related bases to allocate overhead instead of allocating overhead based on a simple, algorithmic basis.

ABC and service organizations

Unlike manufacturing companies, service organizations such as libraries do not produce a physical product.[3] This is no reason, however, not to apply ABC to library computer operations. The logical method of implementing ABC in library operations is first to understand that the various services provided are the product of the library. So, for example, products of an automation department might be commercial and general online reference search services. The next step will be for the library to gather cost information on various functions such as computer maintenance, training and general administration that support the service and allocate them according to the cost drivers that cause them to vary.

WORKED EXAMPLE: TRADITIONAL COSTING VERSUS ABC

Let us assume, as an example, that an information services department provides only three services: general reference; bibliographic instruction and commercial searches.

The costs associated with the department under the traditional method of allocating costs are:

	$
Direct labor	50,000
Direct materials	40,000
Variable overhead	70,000
Fixed overhead	20,000

Under the traditional methods of allocating cost, the entire amount of variable overhead would be allocated using a single basis. For our example, we will use direct labor hours. The relative proportions in each department are:

Reference	10,000 hours = 56%
Bibliographic instruction	6,000 hours = 33%
Commercial searches	2,000 hours = 11%

The following example shows the total costs for each department using this allocation basis:

	Reference	Bibliographic instruction	Commercial searches	Total
	$	$	$	$
Direct labor*	30,000	14,000	6,000	50,000
Direct materials*	18,000	12,000	10,000	40,000
Variable overhead	39,200	23,100	7,700	70,000
Fixed overhead	11,200	6,600	2,200	20,000
Total	98,400	55,700	25,900	180,000

* The numbers here are arbitrary for the purposes of example, but it is assumed that direct materials and labor are known for each department, since these costs are easily traced. Materials include connect time.

A closer analysis of the allocated costs, however, shows that the variable overhead costs can be subdivided into the following cost pools which account for $52,000 of the variable overhead assigned to the department.

	Cost pool $	Reference	Bibliographic instruction	Commercial searches
Administrative costs	16,000			
Number of employees		60	30	10
Repairs	14,000			
Number of machines		50	20	30
Maintenance and cleaning	9,000			
Area (square feet)		2,000	1,500	500
Training	8,000			
Number of employees		60	30	10
Client development	5,000			
Number of billings		0	0	75

Using the relative proportion of each cost driver, the variable overhead costs for the department activities now look like this:

	Cost pool $	Reference $	Bibliographic instruction $	Commercial searches $
Administrative costs (number of employees)	16,000	9,600	4,800	1,600
Repairs (number of machines)	14,000	7,000	2,800	4,200
Maintenance and cleaning area (in square feet)	9,000	4,500	3,375	1,125
Training (number of employees)	8,000	4,800	2,400	800
Client development (number of billings)	5,000	0	0	5,000
Remaining variable overhead (direct labor hours)	18,000	10,080	5,940	1,980
Total	70,000	35,980	19,315	14,705

All amounts are allocated based on the relative proportions of the cost drivers listed in the earlier example. The total costs for the department activities now look like this:

	Reference $	Bibliographic instruction $	Commercial searches $	Total $
Direct labor	30,000	14,000	6,000	50,000
Direct materials	18,000	12,000	10,000	40,000
Variable overhead	35,980	19,315	14,705	70,000
Fixed overhead	11,200	6,600	2,200	20,000
Total	95,180	51,915	32,905	180,000

Note the difference in magnitude between the two methods of allocation:

	$	$	$
Single allocation base	98,400	55,700	25,900
Activity based	95,180	51,915	32,905
Difference	3,300	3,785	7,005

Depending upon the magnitude of the overhead costs and the total costs of the activity, the cost differences between the two systems can be substantial. In the case of the commercial search service, for example, if we assume a level of service at 1000 searches/year, the unit cost for a search changes from $259/search to $329/search, a considerable difference if the department chooses to charge for the service.

THE PROCESS OF ALLOCATION

We have now examined the separate parts of the allocation process:

1   selecting the cost objectives/centers;
2   pooling costs; and
3   choosing allocation bases.

What remains is to implement the allocation process for a given cost center or objective. Once the cost objectives, cost pools and allocation bases have been selected, the following steps should be taken to allocate the costs to a particular department:

1   establish the overhead costs in advance using budgeted or standard costs, rather than actual amounts after the fact;
2   separate the fixed and variable costs in the overhead and allocate each amount separately; and
3   allocate fixed costs on a yearly lump-sum basis based on the capacity that is available to the center/objective.

Allocating costs using this approach will help insure that the decisions made by individual department managers will reflect the true organizational costs of the decisions, not simply the departmental effects.

Allocating costs that reflect true organizational outcomes

Often the process of allocating costs to departments is done in such a way that managers may be encouraged to make decisions that are advantageous to their individual departments but disadvantageous to the organization as a whole. Rather than attempt an abstract explanation, let us examine an example taken from a library to better understand why the above guidelines foster more accurate financial decision-making. To demonstrate this, we offer three approaches to allocating photocopier costs.

WORKED EXAMPLE: PHOTOCOPYING COSTS

We present below the costs and service levels for photocopying activity in a large library.

1 Total copies produced during the year for all depts = 200,000.
2 Assume the following library departments use the copier service and make the following numbers of copies each year:

Circulation	40,000 = 20% of use
Technical services	40,000 = 20% of use
Reference	120,000 = 60% of use

Copy Department total yearly costs are $250,000 of which 15% are variable and 85% are fixed. If we allocate the costs of the copier department based on a proportion of the copies used by each of the other departments the following cost figures would result.

		$
Circulation	20% × $250,000 =	50,000
Technical services	20% × $250,000 =	50,000
Reference	60% × $250,000 =	150,000
		250,000

Imagine the situation, however, if the manager of Circulation makes the decision to look for a cheaper copier service. 'The costs for copier services just keep rising. Why should my department keep absorbing the copier department's costs?' After some searching, he finds a copier service that is willing to fill his copying needs for $45,000 a year. 'I've saved the library $5000/year in copying costs,' he thinks, 'I'll be due for a promotion next year.'

The manager may well be due for promotion since many libraries do not have very sophisticated costing information, but has he really saved the library any money? Let us examine the overall effect on the library of his outsourcing decision.

Assume that the contractor actually supplies all of the copying needs for the Circulation Department. If this occurs, then Circulation's internal consumption of copies drops to zero. The copying department's output then looks as follows:

Total copies	160,000

A decrease of 20%, just as we would expect. The costs, however, look somewhat different.

	$
Fixed costs	212,500
Variable costs	30,000
Total costs of the Copying Department	242,500

The 20% reduction in copier volume has netted only a 3% reduction in costs because most of the costs in the copier department are fixed. The net financial effect on the library is:

	$
Total copier center costs	242,500
Contract copying fees (from the Circulation Department)	45,000
Total library copying costs	287,500

Thus, the attempt by the Circulation Department to reduce its copying costs actually ends up costing the library $37,500 more per year. Moreover, all of the remaining departments will discover that their costs for the following year have risen. Total copies made is now down to 160,000, of course.

Technical services	40,000 = 25% of use
Reference	120,000 = 75% of use

Based on this new copier volume and a new copy center total cost of $242,500, the costs allocated to the remaining departments will look like this:

	$	$
Technical services	25% × 242,500 =	60,625
Reference	75% × 242,500 =	181,875
		242,500

Each of the remaining departments' cost for copying services has risen with no change in their usage. Why should this occur? The difficulty in this case comes from allocating fixed costs in a way that makes them appear to be variable. The managerial challenge in these circumstances is to develop allocation procedures that do not promote departmental actions that are deleterious to the organization as a whole.

Allocation that reflects true costs

We take you through another approach to the photocopy problem to demonstrate an allocation method that reflects true costs.

WORKED EXAMPLE: TRUE COST OF PHOTOCOPYING

The first step in allocating costs that promote overall saving to the library is to divide all of the copier center costs into fixed and variable costs.

	$
Copier center fixed costs	212,500
Copier center variable costs	37,500
Total costs	250,000

The fixed costs can then be assigned as a yearly lump sum to each department based on their anticipated usage. Assuming the same proportions of 20%, 20% and 60% for Circulation, Technical Services and Reference respectively, the yearly fixed costs assigned to each department would be:

	$
Circulation	42,500
Technical Services	42,500
Reference	127,500
	212,500

The remaining variable costs could then be allocated to each department based on their level of consumption. Assuming the same level of copier usage, the projected variable costs for each department would be:

	$
Circulation	7,500
Technical services	7,500
Reference	22,500
	37,500

Under this allocation system, the Circulation Department would still be free to contract out for their copier services, but they will still be required to pay $42,500 for their portion of the fixed copier expenses. Thus, if they made the decision to contract out for their copying needs their total departmental expenses would be:

	$
Fixed allocated costs	42,500
Contract copying fees	45,000
Net copying costs	87,500

The net effect of the manager's decision would be to increase the Circulation Department's net expenses for copying by $37,500. This is exactly the additional expense that would have accrued to the library under the old system. However, the effects of the decision are limited to the department that makes the decision. Outsourcing the copying service no longer has an impact on Reference or Technical Services.

The key to allocating expenses that are limited to department/cost centers is to make the allocation decisions based on the behavior of the costs. Costs should be divided into fixed and variable costs and allocated separately based on these categories.

Allocating costs to services

Until now, we have concerned ourselves only with the transfer of costs from one internal department to another. At some point, however, we need to determine the cost of providing our final product, which in the case of libraries is usually the provision of services to users. The flow of costs and services in a library, for examples may be as represented by columns in Table 3.1.

Table 3.1 Flow of costs and services in a library

Internal services ⟶	Public services ⟶	Library output
Library administration	Reference	Services to the
Maintenance	Circulation	public
Security	Children's programs	
Acquisitions	Adult programs	
Technical services	Commercial programs	
Automation services		

Costs and services could flow in several different directions. Service departments, for example, provide services to each other as well to public services while library administration processes payroll for acquisitions, and so on.

Internal service costs make their way to the public service departments of the library and ultimately to the cost of services or other products that constitute the library's output. The allocation basis use for transferring internal costs to public service departments is the one that best measures the value of the services rendered to those departments.

Accounting texts discuss a number of methods of linking costs to output. Two widely-used and easily understood methods will be described here. They are **direct allocation** and **step-down alloca-**

tion. A third method, reciprocal allocation, is also widely used but it is significantly more complex than most practitioners require.

For simplicity's sake, the following discussions will use only two service departments, each with a single allocation basis, and will ignore any distinction between fixed and variable costs.

Method one: direct allocation

Direct allocation is the easier of the two methods to implement, and as a result has been widely adopted in many organizations. It ignores services rendered by one support service department to another and allocates each support service department's costs entirely to the service-producing departments.

WORKED EXAMPLE: DIRECT ALLOCATION

The Automation Services Department has a yearly budget of $100,000. The costs of the department are allocated based on the number of processing hours (out of a total of 6000) used by each public services department. The estimated number of processing hours for each department is as follows:

Circulation:	3000 = 50% (3000/6,000)
Reference:	1500 = 25% (1500/6,000)
Commercial services	1500 = 25% (1200/6,000)

The Maintenance Department has a yearly budget of $75,000. Its costs are allocated based on the number of square feet (out of a total of 25,000) each department occupies. The area for each department is as follows:

Automation services	5,000
Circulation	8,000 = 40% (8,000/20,000)
Reference	10,000 = 50% (10,000/20,000)
Commercial services	2,000 = 10% (2,000/20,000)

Though the total area of the library is 25,000 square feet under the direct allocation method, Maintenance does not allocate its costs to Automation Services. In order to accurately allocate maintenance costs to the remaining departments, the areas occupied by circulation, reference and commercial services are divided by 20,000, the total area that the service-producing departments occupy. Direct allocations are as follows.

	Automation Department	Maintenance Department	Circulation Department	Reference Department	Commercial	Total
	$	$	$	$	$	$
Predicted overhead before allocation	100,000	75,000	230,000	280,000	110,000	795,000
Allocation						
Automation costs	(100,000)		50,000	25,000	25,000	
Maintenance		(75,000)	30,000	37,500	7,500	
Total	0	0	310,000	342,500	142,500	795,000

At the conclusion of the process, all the expenses for both Maintenance and Automation Services are completely allocated to the public service departments. Note that none of the expenses of maintenance were allocated to Automation Services (or vice versa) although it is likely that these departments may perform services for each other.

In some organizations, failing to recognize the reciprocal nature of services among internal departments may create significant distortions in costing. For this reason, direct costing is often not sufficient as a method of allocating costs. In such cases, the step-down costing method may be required to give an acceptably accurate picture of departmental costs.

Method two: step-down costing

Step-down costing requires each department to allocate its costs to all of the remaining departments in the organization regardless of whether they produce a service or product. Each department allocates its total costs, in turn, until all of the organizational costs are passed on to the final products or services. As each department's costs are allocated, the total costs of the department are reduced to zero and the department ceases to be part of the allocation process.

The general rule for the order of allocation is to begin with the department that provides service for the greatest number of other departments and proceed from there in order of service provision. In our library example, it would be more plausible to begin with Maintenance, since its services are likely to be used by the greatest number of departments in the organization. The method provides a more accurate picture of actual resource use in the organization, though some distortion still remains since Automation Services may provide a service to maintenance that is not taken into account. Using the same set of costs as in our earlier direct costing example, the step-down costs of the library would look rather different.

WORKED EXAMPLE: STEP-DOWN COSTING

Since maintenance costs are now allocated to all of the remaining departments, the allocation is now based on the total area of 25,000 square feet less the 5000 square feet occupied by Automation Services and the 20,000 square feet that the Circulation, Reference and Commercial Services departments occupy. The new allocations of the total square footage costs for each department are:

Automation Services	5,000 = 20% (5,000/25,000)
Circulation:	8,000 = 32% (8,000/25,000)
Reference:	10,000 = 40% (10,000/25,000)
Commercial Services:	2,000 = 8% (2,000/20,000)

Note that the allocation basis for Automation Services does not change since it still allocates its costs to the same service departments in the same proportion as in the direct allocation method. Step-down allocations are as follows.

	Maintenance Department	Automation Department	Circulation Department	Reference Department	Commercial Department	Total
	$	$	$	$	$	$
Predicted overhead before allocation	75,000	100,000	230,000	280,000	110,000	795,000
First step-down allocation (Maintenance Department)	(75,000)	15,000	24,000	30,000	6,000	
Total expenses after 1st allocation	0	115,000	254,000	310,000	116,000	
Second step-down allocation (Automation Department)	0	(115,000)	57,500	28,750	28,750	
Total	0	0	311,500	338,750	144,750	795,000

Compare the costs of the service departments between the two allocation methods:

	Circulation Department $	Reference Department $	Commercial Department $
Direct allocation	310,000	342,500	142,500
Step-down allocation	–311,500	–338,750	–144,750
Difference	(1,500)	3,750	(2,250)

The reference department's costs were reported at $3750 more with the direct distribution method, while circulation and commercial service were reported respectively at $1500 and $2250. Depending on the magnitude and nature of the costs being allocated, the distortion that is caused by direct allocation can be significant.

Other more complicated allocation methods can be used that remove most of the distortion that remains with standard step-down costing. The most common methods are double distribution and reciprocal, or matrix, distribution. While these methods produce greater accuracy in allocating costs, they are also significantly more complicated to perform and understand. In most cases, a step-down allocation should be sufficiently accurate. Readers interested in pursuing this subject are referred to the cost accounting texts in the references section at the end of this chapter.

STANDARD COSTS AND MANAGERIAL CONTROL

A final purpose of allocated costs that will be covered in this chapter is their use in developing standard costs. Allocated costs form a large, but not exclusive part of standard costs.

Standard costs defined

Standards may be defined as criteria or benchmarks against which performance can be measured. Standard costs are predetermined levels of what it should cost to produce a unit of a given product or service. The inputting of a record into an OPAC, for example, may have a standard cost of $3.82 which includes the direct labor, materials and overhead necessary to place a single record into the system.

Why use standard costs?

The use of standard costs provides a number of benefits to managers.

1   Easier, cheaper costing. Standard costs can provide financial information that represents product/services costs as well as actual historical cost data, but is cheaper, easier and faster to gather.

2   Delegating responsibility while maintaining control is easier. With accurate service cost figures, managers and employees can become more cost conscious and more economical in their work. Standards allow self-correction at lower levels in the organization. Management by 'exception' (see below) frees upper management from intervening in cost matters unless they exceed pre-determined limits.

Developing standard costs

Setting standards begins with the selection of a relevant product or service. A computer manufacturing firm, for example, would probably be interested in knowing the standard costs for assembling each of the printed circuit boards used in its machines. Libraries are less likely to produce physical products, but they may be interested in knowing the standard costs for performing a variety of the public services that are, in effect, their products. Possible areas for setting standards might include, but are not limited to, data entry, acquisitions (the cost of ordering or processing a book), circulation (inputting a new user, sending out overdue notices), or online searching (the cost of a user search). The basis for selecting a product or service should have some relevance to understanding the financial performance of the organization.

Once a service has been selected both its costs and its levels of output need to be estimated. Both costs and output should be in accordance with historical information, but estimates need to go beyond simple historical costs. Standards should be a reflection of how production should have occurred as well as what actually occurred. In practice, this may mean consultation with a number of technical managers such as the systems librarian for data entry questions. Poor and/or unreasonable standards are often the result of setting standards based only on meetings with upper management and excluding managers in charge of day-to-day operations.

There is some controversy among managers concerning whether standards should be ideal or practical. Ideal standards are usually defined as those that can be met only under the best conditions. Proponents of ideal standards cite the 'pull' aspects of very high standards as motivational standards. Very few organizations use ideal standards. Critics of this approach note that under it, employees need guidance on what their work may reasonably be. Standards that can rarely or never be met are of little use.

Practical standards, on the other hand, may be described as 'tight but reasonable'. That is, the standard may be reasonably achieved by a highly efficient and motivated worker. Variances from practical standards (i.e. more or less expense for the same unit) usually provide better information to managers since they indicate a difference in cost from what a normal, efficient worker would produce. Ideal standards, however, rarely are achieved, so that shortfalls from these standards are commonplace. As a result, ideal standards have little value to a manager either in diagnosing problems or in planning anticipated cash flows or costs.

Once a standard for the standard (ideal or practical) has been decided, the manager estimates first the relevant level of output for the product or service and then the accompanying costs. The usual component costs for a standard cost are:

1 direct labor;
2 direct materials;
3 departmental indirect costs (fixed and variable); and
4 allocated costs from other departments (fixed and variable).

For the purpose of simplifying the following example, the techniques by which the costs from other departments are allocated will not be discussed. Methods of allocating costs are covered in detail in Chapter 4.

WORKED EXAMPLE: DERIVING STANDARD COSTS

Assume that the Technical Services Department estimates that for the coming year it can expect to input 20,000 records. The department estimates that it will incur the following costs at this level of service.

To input one record		$
Direct labor		
10 minutes @ $12/hour		2.00
Direct materials [1]		
Forms and paper	0.20	
Online connect time (5 minutes @ $36/hour)	3.00	
Total materials		5.20
Technical Services Department indirect costs		
Variable (labor, etc.)		2.50
Fixed (salaries, depreciation, training, etc.)		
$50,000 divided by expected level of service = 20,000		2.50
Allocated from other Departments		
Variable		1.00
Fixed		
$22,000 divided by expected level of service = 20,000		1.10
Standard cost to input one record		12.30

1. Physical materials are probably a minor cost, but it is also reasonable to include the cost of services, such as connect time to a database, which are paid for as they are used. A more helpful and accurate term for automated services might be 'Resources consumed'.

It may be useful in this context to think of standard costs as analogous to budgets, except that they are concerned with unit costs rather than organizational costs. That is, a standard cost is the budget needed to produce one item of product or service.

VARIANCE ANALYSIS AND MANAGEMENT BY EXCEPTION

Managers typically make decisions concerning inputs to the production of services that involve two variables: the price of inputs and the quantity of inputs. The use of standard costs allows managers to assess the performance of a department by comparing the budgeted costs and quantities of inputs used to provide a particular level of output with the actual costs of providing that output.

We can think of variance analysis occurring at various levels of detail, the most basic of which is the comparison of a static budget with the actual costs of producing units of service or products at some level of service. Comparison against static budgets is the easiest variance analysis to perform, but it also provides the least useful information to managers. Static budgets are limited to a single level of production or service that may not be reflected by the actual budget amounts. The following is an example of a static budget variance analysis.

WORKED EXAMPLE: STATIC BUDGET VARIANCE ANALYSIS

	Actual	Budgeted	Variance
Records input	20,000	18,000	
Variable costs			
Direct labor	$40,000	$38,000	$2,000 (U)
Direct materials (total)	$64,000	$62,000	$2,000 (F)
Variable overhead (total)	$70,000	$68,000	$2,000 (U)
Fixed expenses	$70,000	$70,000	
Total variance			$2,000 (U)

Variances may be either **favorable** (F) if they are lower than the budget predicted or **unfavorable** (U) if they are higher than predicted. The comparison is normally made on a line by line basis. Note that the actual costs in the example differ from the budgeted amounts. The actual level of service, however, is higher than the budgeted level of service. Thus, it becomes problematic to determine if the budget variances are the result of price increases, poor management, or simply changes in production volumes.

Using standard costs allows us to develop flexible budgets which may be defined as budgets that account for various levels of service with cost amounts that also vary with the level of service. The variance analysis then compares aggregate costs for a given time period. The following example uses the same data derived for the standard costs of inputting records by the Technical Services Department.

WORKED EXAMPLE: FLEXIBLE BUDGET VARIANCE ANALYSIS

	Actual	Budgeted	Variance
Records input	20,000	20,000	
Variable costs			
Direct labor	$43,000	$40,000	$3,000 (U)
Direct materials (total)	$62,000	$64,000	$2,000 (F)
Variable overhead (total)	$69,000	$70,000	$1,000 (F)
Fixed expenses	$71,000	$70,000	$1,000 (U)
Total variance			$1,000 (U)

The flexible budget used in the example can be adjusted for changes in the volume of output. Note that the unit prices for costs remain constant in the budget so that the variance analysis focuses on the effects of changes in volume at the aggregate level.

Variances can be calculated in much greater detail for any of the variable inputs – direct labor, direct materials and variable overhead – providing that standard costs have been derived for them. The illustration below provides a general model for calculating variances in costs and quantity.

1   Actual unit quantity ×
        Actual unit price

                                        Price variances
                                        1–2
2   Actual unit quantity ×   Budget variance
        Standard unit price   1–3
                                    Efficiency variances
3   Standard unit quantity ×   2 –3
        Standard unit price

Price variances are calculated by taking the difference between the actual price of an input and the budgeted price of an input, multiplied by the number of output units produced.

Efficiency variances are calculated by taking the difference between the actual quantity of an input and the budgeted quantity of an input needed to achieve some actual level of output and multiplying it by a budgeted unit price.

The following examples will help illustrate how variances are calculated for various inputs. The examples all use the standard costs for technical services data input and assume a budgeted output of 20,000 records entered.

WORKED EXAMPLE: PRICE VARIANCES

Input	Budgeted price	Actual price	Variance
Direct labor	$40,000	$50,000	$10,000 (U)
	$2.00 × 20,000	$2.50 × 20,000	
	(based on a rate of	(based on a rate of	
	10 minutes	10 minutes	
	@ $12/hour to	@ $15/hour to	
	input 1 record)	input 1 record)	
Direct materials	$64,000	$64,000	0
Variable overhead	$70,000	$65,000	$5,000 (F)
	(($1 + 2.50) × 20,000)	(($.75 + 2.50) × 20,000)	

WORKED EXAMPLE: EFFICIENCY VARIANCES

Input	Budgeted usage	Actual usage	Variance
Direct labor	$40,000	$48,000	$8,000 (U)
	$2 ×20,000	$2.40 ×20,000	
	(based on a rate of	(based on a rate of	
	10 minutes.	12 minutes	
	@ $12/hour to	@ $12/hour	
	input 1 record)	to input 1 record)	
Direct Materials	$64,000	$88,000*	$14,000 (U)
	(3.20 × 20,000)	(4.40 × 20,000)	

* Rate reflects an increase in the actual amount of connect time used:

Forms and paper	$0.20
Online connect time (7 minutes @ $36/hour)	$4.20
Total materials	$4.40

MANAGEMENT BY EXCEPTION USING STANDARD COSTS

An advantage of using standard costs is that upper level managers can delegate cost responsibility to their subordinates and intervene only when the variances exceed certain pre-determined limits (i.e. the 'exceptions' of management by exception). Upper management can easily delegate responsibilities yet remain informed of serious cost problems in costs as they develop.

When to intervene

Standard costs are developed based on estimates of resource use for the production of services. Since no estimate will predict activity perfectly, some variance is inevitable. Since every variance should not be considered an exception, the question management must answer is, when does a variance cause an exception? In general terms, the answer might be at a level high enough to indicate a problem is likely, but not so high as to have allowed a crisis to occur. In practice, the level will need to be negotiated individually, but four criteria can be used to assess when to intervene.

1   Materiality. How big is the variance? Since some variance is inevitable, management does not need to be informed every time the actual cost differs from the budgeted cost. Often, management sets some benchmark that the variance must exceed before an exception is generated. For example, a benchmark for direct labor may be that any difference that does not exceed 15% of the budgeted amount does not generate an exception report.

2   Ability of the manager to control the cost. As we discussed earlier, some cost variances are beyond the control of individual managers. Rates for electricity may increase during a budget period, for example, but they will require little intervention since they are beyond managerial control. These variances may still be listed in departmental exception reports as an indication to upper management that costs will increase, but little follow-up work may result.

3   Frequency with which the variance occurs. Regardless of their magnitude, variances that occur consistently in the same areas may be a concern for management scrutiny. Frequent variances from an established standard may indicate that the standard is out of date or lax management practices, both of which require intervention.

4   Centrality of the cost. Some items are so integral to an activity that changes in their costs are of material interest even if they occur for the first time or are out of the manager's control. Connect time, for example, is such a large portion of the record input cost, that knowing when changes in the connection rate occur is of material importance in running the department.

What exceptions tell management

Remember that exceptions tell managers only that something unexpected has occurred with regard to costs, not what has caused the exception. Standards are based on estimates, and an exception may indicate a need to estimate more accurately rather than poor management. Similarly, the total cost of providing a service has many components, some or all of which may not be within the control of a manager. Exception reports indicate that more information is needed, not that a manager needs to be disciplined.

REFERENCES

1   McClure, C. R., 'User-based data collection techniques and strategies for evaluating networked information services', *Library trends*, **42** (4), 1994, 591–607.

2   Cooper, R., Kaplan, R., Maisel, L., Morrissey, E. and Oehm, R., *Implementing activity-based cost management: moving from analysis to action*, Institute of Management Accountants, Montvale, NJ, 1992.

3   Pirrong, G., 'As easy as ABC: Using activity based costing in service industries', *The national public accountant*, **30** (2), 1993, 22–6.

CHAPTER 4

Threading your way through capital investment decisions

The following scenario illustrates some of the difficulties of making good investment decisions.

SCENARIO

Arthur Jones, the Librarian of Princes College Library faces a number of investment decisions for the approaching fiscal year. The first of these decisions relates to photocopiers. Over the past six months, the five photocopiers which serve the main library, purchased five years ago, have become increasingly unreliable. They have been out of warranty for the past 18 months. Discussions with the previous supplier and other vendors have begun, and estimates requested for options on leasing and purchase, with varying warranty periods.

'How do I choose the right option from all these salesmen's' claims?', he wonders. 'Is it a good idea to pay $4800 for a copier that earns us $1500 a year in revenue if another costs $4990 and earns a $1100 in years 1 and 2 and $1500 in three years?'

'I wouldn't mind deciding that one by flipping a coin. Should I purchase or should I lease? One company wants us to buy the system for $14,000 and to pay for all our own maintenance. Another wants us to lease the system for $4500 a year over the next four years. The second one looks more expensive, but I'm sure it can't be that simple. The online reserve system is even worse. I'm sure we're bleeding capital to keep it going, but I can't see where and how the money goes.'

'My financial manager is worse than useless. I asked him for help and he starts babbling about discounting cashflows and present value. Somehow it appears that the $4500 lease payment I

*will have to make in three years' time will be worth $3888 now.
Idiot. How can a $4500 payment ever be less than $4500?'*

*Worse still, it looks as though I've got to close one of the depart-
ments where we're charging the business community for services.
I can't understand how it can happen, but it looks as though one
of them is losing money. If I could just see where things are
falling short, we might continue the services.'*

As we can see, the librarian at Princes College is thus faced with a
range of capital investment and financial evaluation decisions, with
very little guidance to help him. We discuss below some techniques
that may allow him to prioritize his decisions and capitalize most
effectively on his investments. The chapter begins by discussing
which criteria are relevant for making investment decisions and con-
tinues from there to discuss a variety of techniques for decision-
making including contribution margin analysis and payback and
present value analysis.

RELEVANT COSTS

What costs are relevant in making investment decisions? The
answer is that all costs associated with an investment option are relevant except:

1 sunk costs; and
2 costs which do not differ among investment options.

Since investment decisions must necessarily involve the future,
costs which we have already incurred and cannot be recovered (i.e.
sunk costs) are not relevant to the decision. However, not all future
costs are relevant to the decision either. Only those costs which differ among options should be included in the decision process. Costs
which will be incurred regardless of which investment is made
should not enter into the decision.

Identifying relevant costs

There is a natural tendency among managers to include sunk costs as part of the decision process for new investments. This is a natural tendency because we are generally reluctant to decide that money we have already spent may not provide the best investment solutions. Let us illustrate this by an example.

WORKED EXAMPLE: THE DECISION TO UPDATE

Princes Library has purchased a CD-ROM jukebox and LAN system for $12,000. A second system comes on the market after it has made the initial purchase which requires additional capital outlay and disposing of the old system. The new system is, however, significantly cheaper to operate. The costs associated with the systems are as follows. Assume a useful life of four years for each alternative.

Option 1		Option 2	
Purchase price	$12,000	Purchase price	
Current resale value	$2,000	(additional investment)	$14,000
Yearly operating costs	$9,000	Yearly operating costs	$3,000

The initial reaction of many managers when confronted with this choice is not to make the investment in Option 2 since that would mean a 'loss' of $10,000 ($12,000–$10,000) on the resale of the system that has already been purchased. It is tempting to assert that the organization needs to use the system in 'order to get back the money they already spent'. However, keeping the old system is less financially advantageous than purchasing the new one. We demonstrate this via the following example showing differential costs.

	Use old system $	Buy new system $	Difference $
Purchase costs	0	14,000	14,000
Yearly operating costs	36,000	12,000	(24,000)
Depreciation on old system/loss write-off	10,000	10,000	0
Salvage value old system	0	(2,000)	(2,000)
Total costs (4 years)	46,000	34,000	(12,000)

Notice that the remaining salvage value of the old machine had no effect on the decision. The $10,000 leaves the organization either in the form of depreciation from using the machine or as the result of writing off the loss. In either case the organization absorbs the residual $10,000 value of the old machine.

What then, were the relevant costs in this case? Using the guidelines we established earlier, the following costs should have been eliminated:

1 Sunk costs

	$
The original purchase price of the old system	12,000
The remaining value of the machine after resale	10,000

2 Costs which do not differ among investment options
   Operating costs (to the extent of the common $12,000)

Whatever costs are left will form the basis for making the investment decision.

	$
Yearly savings produced by new system	
(4 years x $6,000/year)	24,000
Additional purchase cost of new system	(14,000)
Salvage value of old system	2,000
Net savings of new system	12,000

Note that the result of this analysis is exactly the same as that found in the difference column in the earlier part of this example.

Differential costs and allocated fixed costs

We have already observed that future costs that do not differ among investment alternatives have no bearing on investment decisions. If the organization must incur the costs regardless of whether an investment is made or not, then the costs are irrelevant. This principle is easily put into effect when there are only direct costs, but can become problematic in organizations that allocate organizational fixed costs to departments as in the following example of an actual corporate library.

WORKED EXAMPLE: FIXED AND VARIABLE COSTS (1)

XYZ Corporation maintained a small corporate information center. The center was operated as a cost center which was financed through payments by corporate departments. The following monthly cost information is associated with the center:

	$	$
Monthly revenue		4400
Direct labor	1500	
Direct materials/services	1200	
Allocated building overhead	2000	
Net profit (loss) of center		(1300)

Based on this analysis, the corporation made an initial decision to close the center since it was operating at a loss. On closer examination it became clear that the organization was better off with the center operating and the decision was reversed. We can demonstrate this through the following analysis:

Total monthly costs for the building:

	Information center operating $	Information center closed $
Variable costs	2,700	0
Fixed costs (total for building)	20,000	20,000
Less revenue	(4,400)	0
Total monthly expenses	18,300	20,000

The center was actually covering its variable expenses and contributing an additional $1700 toward the fixed expenses of the building. The net effect of closing the center is a loss to the building expenses of $1700.

The cause is allocating fixed expenses in a manner that makes them appear to be variable and then forgetting that they are fixed. The allocated expenses do not disappear when the program is closed. In order to guard against mistakes of this sort when making investment decisions a useful technique is what is known as the contribution margin approach.

Contribution margin and investment alternatives

The contribution margin approach examines systems or programs in the context of if and how well they cover or exceed their variable costs.

WORKED EXAMPLE: FIXED AND VARIABLE COSTS (2)

Princes Library has three departments that generate revenue. The revenues and variable expenses are known for each of the departments and the fixed expenses have been allocated based on floor space. The associated revenues and expenses for each department are as follows.

	Business Reference Department $00	Online Services Department $00	Copying Services Department $00	Total $00
Revenue	110	100	80	290
variable costs	75	70	65	210
fixed costs	25	15	20	60
Total costs	100	85	85	270
Net profit/(loss)	10	15	(5)	20

Based on this analysis, it would appear that the library should close the copying services department since it appears to be a money-loser. However, let us examine the net effect that closing the department has on the organization as a whole:

	Copying services open $000		Copying services closed $000	
Revenue		290		210
Less variable costs	210		145	
Less fixed costs	60		60	
Total costs		(270)		(205)
Net profit/(loss)		20		5

As we can see, closing the department has a net effect of losing the organization money. The problem that this example illustrates comes from allocating expenses to a department in way that makes them appear to be variable. As we have discussed earlier, there may be good managerial reasons for allocating costs in this manner, but the danger is that you may forget that allocated fixed costs do not disappear even if the program/system has been eliminated. This oversight can lead to poor managerial decisions and decisions to reduce or remove programs that actually make money for the organization.

A better approach to decision-making results from evaluating each program individually to determine to what extent it covers its variable costs and contributes to the organization's fixed costs.

WORKED EXAMPLE: CONTRIBUTION APPROACH TO PROGRAM EVALUATION

	Business Reference Department $000	Online Services Department $000	Copying Services Department $000	Total $000
Revenue	110	100	80	290
Less variable costs	75	70	65	210
Contribution to fixed costs	35	30	15	80
Less fixed costs				60
Net profit/(loss)				20

We can now evaluate each program for the possible effects of eliminating it, based on its contribution to the organization as a whole. Similarly, we make the same decisions for adding a system or service based on its ability to cover its own variable costs.

This is not to say that fixed costs have no bearing in the decision process. As we know, costs remain fixed only for a relevant range of activities. However, by examining the contribution of individual programs we are better able to see which of a range of investment options take best advantage of the limited capacity of our fixed expenses.

The utility of allocating fixed expenses to a program also depends upon whether the organization is evaluating programs or pricing them. It makes little sense to evaluate programs based on allocated costs, since the manager has no control over them (see Chapter 3 for a more detailed discussion of the problems of evaluating cost centers using allocated costs). The same may not be true in the case of pricing services. Since a given service cannot exist without the supporting organization, it can be argued that an outside user should bear part of the cost. (Chapter 5 discusses this and other pricing issues at greater length.)

DECISION-MAKING TECHNIQUES

Technique I: Payback analysis

Payback analysis is a measure of the time that it takes to repay the initial investment in an asset or program. Given an initial outlay of capital and a projected set of uniform cash-flows, payback provides an estimate of how soon an investment will repay its initial costs. The equation to calculate a payback period takes the general form:

$$\text{Payback period} = \frac{\text{Incremental capital investment}}{\text{Yearly cash inflow from investment}}$$

WORKED EXAMPLE: PAYBACK AND UNIFORM CASH-FLOW

Princes College library purchases a copy machine for $3900. The machine is expected to generate an average of $1400 in copier revenues each year from patrons. What is the payback period?

$$P = \frac{3900}{1400}$$

= 2.79 years (rounded up)

Payback and non-uniform cashflows

The equation above deals with payback in situations which have a uniform cash inflow. Many investments, however, generate a stream of irregular payments. In such cases, payback must be calculated on an incremental basis.

WORKED EXAMPLE: PAYBACK AND NON-UNIFORM CASHFLOW

Assume the same copier price of $3900. Instead of a regular stream of payments, however, cash inflows are expected to be low at first, rise for several years as the public becomes more accustomed to the service and then level off. The revenue stream is predicted as follows.

	Revenue	Accumulated revenue
	$	$
Year 1	950	950
Year 2	1100	2050
Year 3	1250	3300
Year 4	1890	5190
Year 5	1890	7080

Payback occurs slightly beyond the third year. The final $600 needed to complete the payback ($3900–$3300) indicates that the total payback period is 3.32 years (3 years + 600 = 3.32 years). That is, the investment is paid back slightly less than one-third of the way into Year 4.

Payback and risk

The simple method of payback analysis answers the question: What is the payback period if operations go as expected? Often, however, projects have varying degrees of risk. In such cases it also becomes important to address the question of: which investment offers the best protection if something should go wrong and we are forced to abandon the project? The analysis of payback that concerns risk is usually known as the 'bailout payback' period.

In such cases, the salvage value of the investment as well as the payback need to be taken into account. In particular, it is useful to recall that special-purpose equipment is usually difficult to resell and has a faster depreciation rate than more general purpose equipment.

WORKED EXAMPLE: SIMPLE AND BAILOUT PAYBACK ANALYSIS

A simpler version of the decision facing Princes Library would be having to choose between buying two copy machines for public use. Copy machine 1 is more specialized and costs more, but has the potential to generate more revenue for the library. Copy machine 2 costs less, generates revenue more slowly, but also deteriorates more slowly and is easier to resell. The costs and revenues for each machine are as follows:

	Copy machine 1		Copy machine 2
	$		$
Purchase price	10,000	Purchase price	6,000
Yearly revenue	2,500	Yearly revenue	1,200
Salvage value after		Salvage value after	
Year 1	6,000	Year 1	4,500
Year 2	4,500	Year 2	3,600
Year 3	3,000	Year 3	2,400
Year 4	1,500	Year 4	1,200

Traditional payback: the project works as well as planned.

Option 1   Option 2

P = $10,000 ÷ 4 years   P = $6000 ÷ 5 years
  = $2500   = $1200

Bailout payback: the project does not work as well as planned.

Year ending	Cumulative revenue	Salvage value	Cumulative total
	$	$	$
Option 1			
Year 1	2,500	6,000	8,500
Year 2	5,000	4,500	9,000
Year 3	7,500	3,000	10,500
Option 2			
Year 1	1,200	4,500	5,700
Year 2	2,400	3,600	6,000

In the case of bailout payback analysis, Option 1 allows the organization to recover its investment between Years 2 and 3 while Option 2 allows recovery at the end of Year 2. Note how the different interpretations of payback yield different results. Traditional payback analysis indicates that the first option repays its investment more quickly. If the organization's intention is to minimize risk, though, then the second option is clearly better. This technique can be extended to as many options as the organization needs to consider and/or has the resources to cost out. Similarly, this method can be used for the purchase of multiple units as in the case of Princes Library's five copiers.

Strengths and limitations of payback analysis

Payback analysis is best used in situations where managers have a large number of investment options to assess in a short period of time; and when projects are extremely risky. Payback analysis, while easy to perform, has two serious flaws as a decision-making technique. The first is that its reliance on the minimum period for return on investment biases decisions in favor of short-term gains at the expense of long-term profitability or savings. A second problem is that the technique does not adequately address the timing of payments and the time value of money. The remainder of this chapter deals with the time value of money and its use in investment decisions.

Technique 2: Present value analysis

The time value of money

The value of money does not remain constant over time. A familiar example of this is the compound interest earned in a savings account. Money that is placed on deposit today will have a higher value in the future as a result of the interest it accrues. The money accrues interest not only on the original amount deposited (known in finance as the principal) but also on the accrued interest that is redeposited – the 'compounding' portion of compound interest.

In finance terms, this higher value is referred to as **future value** (FV) and it can be computed using the following formula.

Future Value = Principal × (1+ interest rate) period on deposit

WORKED EXAMPLE: FUTURE VALUE

Imagine that you have placed $5000 on deposit for three years in a savings account that bears 5% interest. The future value of the $5000 would be calculated as follows:

Principal	$5000
Interest rate	5% (or 0.05)
Years on deposit	3

FV = $5000 $(1+0.05)^3$ = $5000 × 1.16 = $5800

That is, at the end of the third year your original 5000 would have grown to $5800. Conversely, money that you will receive or pay in the future has a lower value today than money that you actually have in your possession. People who are new to finance often have trouble, at first, understanding how the value of a future payment or revenue could ever be less than its face value: 'I still have to pay out $2000 in three years'; they say, 'so I don't see why it should be worth any less today.'

There are several ways to conceptualize why monies paid or received in the future are worth less than their face value today.

1   A future payment requires less money on hand than the amount of the future payment. In other words, if you have to pay someone $1000 in three years' time you don't have to have $1000 on hand today. Assuming a 3% interest rate on savings accounts, you would only need to deposit $917 (rounded to the nearest dollar) today to have $1000 in three years. This is the principle at work in bonds or savings certificates which are redeemable for a specified face amount at a future date but which are sold for less than the face amount before that date is reached.

2   During the period between the present and the future time for payment, the recipient loses the benefit of having the funds. Let us use our earlier future value illustration as an example and imagine that you have signed an agreement to pay $5000 at the end of three years. During the three-year period, the recipient loses $800 that he or she might have received by investing the funds. The loss of value does not only happen in cases where the recipient would or could have invested the funds. A reduction in value may occur because of the need to borrow as a result of not having the money available or through the loss of alternative uses of the money (usually defined as the opportunity cost).

3   The longer the period between the present and the time of payment, the greater is the risk that the money will not be paid. Some arrangements are significantly more or less risky than others, but there is always the chance in any transaction that a payment may not be made if only through acts of God, war, or the

death of the principles. Risk is often difficult to quantify, but it is a cost.

In finance terms, the lower value that funds paid in the future have today is known as **present value**. The equation used to calculate future value is the corollary of that used for present value:

$$\text{Present Value} = \frac{\text{Principal}}{(1 + \text{interest rate})^{\text{periods before payment}}}$$

WORKED EXAMPLE: PRESENT VALUE

Principal	$5000
Interest rate	5% (or 0.05)
Years before payment	3

$$PV = \frac{\$5000}{(1+0.05)^3} = \frac{\$5000}{1.16} = \$4310$$

In the case of present value, the interest rate is referred to as the **discount rate** or cost of capital. This is the price that the organization pays to use money. Borrowing rates are useful as the starting point for determining the discount rate, but the concept involves more than loans. Determining the discount rate for an organization is discussed in greater detail later in this chapter.

It is simple to calculate PV using the formula; if you intend to set up a PV calculation on a spreadsheet program it may be necessary to enter the equation if the spreadsheet does not have built-in present value functions. However, present value calculations are made so often in finance management that tables, consisting of precalculated present values for various periods and discount rates, are frequently used.

The tables are calculated for the amount of $1.00. To obtain the present value of any other amount, simply multiply the principal by the amount on the table.

Table 4.1 Present value of a lump sum

Periods	5%	6%	7%	8%	9%	10%	12%	14%
1	.952	.943	.935	.926	.917	.909	.983	.877
2	.907	.890	.873	.857	.842	.826	.797	.769
3	.864	.840	.816	.794	.772	.751	.712	.675
4	.823	.792	.763	.735	.708	.683	.636	.592
5	.784	.747	.713	.681	.650	.621	.567	.519
6	.746	.705	.666	.630	.596	.565	.507	.456
7	.711	.665	.623	.584	.547	.513	.452	.399
8	.677	.627	.582	.540	.502	.467	.404	.351
9	.645	.592	.544	.500	.460	.424	.361	.308
10	.614	.558	.508	.463	.422	.386	.322	.270

WORKED EXAMPLE: USE OF PV TABLES

Problem
What is the PV of $247 due in three years at a discount rate of 6%?

Solution
To find the answer begin by looking down the left column marked, 'Periods' until you come to 3. Then look across until you come the column marked 6%. The number there should be .842. To get the PV of $247, multiply .842 x 247 = $208.

Tables included in this book are for a limited range of discount rates and periods only. Present value tables for a wider range of rates and periods are available in most accounting and finance textbooks and as separate reference volumes (see the list of references at the end of the chapter for examples). The tables can also be set up quickly using a spreadsheet.

Annuities

The example we have just looked at is known as a lump sum; that is, a single payment paid at one time in the future. It is also usual in financial transactions to have a steady stream of payments made at regular intervals. In finance, these payments are known as annuities. In order for a stream of payments to be an annuity, they must meet the following conditions:

1 the payment must begin in the first period of the payback time; and

2 the amount of the payment must be same in each period.

It is important to keep these conditions in mind because they will affect how the present value of the payments is calculated.

The following payments are annuities: $1000 per year for five years; and $1000 per year in Years 1–3 and $2000 per year in Years 4–5. Only Years 1–3 can be treated as an annuity, since it is only for this period that the two conditions are met.

These, however, are not annuities: $1000 in Year 1; $1200 in Year 2; and $1005 in Year 3; or $1000 in Year 1; and $2000 per year in Years 2–5. A common mistake in the latter example is to treat the last four years as a four-year annuity. This leads to an incorrect answer as demonstrated below.

Calculating the present value of annuities

Annuities are calculated by adding together the present values of individual lump sums, as the following worked example shows.

WORKED EXAMPLE: PRESENT VALUE OF ANNUITIES

Assume that you have signed a lease agreement that requires you to pay for a copy machine according to the following terms: a 5% discount rate; a 3-year lease period; a $1000/year lease payment; and payments to be made at the end of each year. The yearly lump sums look like this:

$1000 × .952 = $952
$1000 × .907 = $907
$1000 × .864 = $864
$2.723 $2723

Thus, the present value of the lease payments is $2723. Because the annuities are calculated so frequently, tables with the present values precalculated are also commonly used. As with lump sums, the amounts are calculated for yearly payments of $1.00. In order to find the present value of an annuity, we simply look down the left side of the table to find the number of periods (3 in this case) and then look across the table until we find the correct interest rate (5%). The value in table 4.2 is

2.723, the same number we get when we add each individual lump sum. In order to arrive at the present value for the annuity, the amount from the table is multiplied by the yearly annuity payment – $1000.00 in our example.

Table 4.2 Present value of an ordinary annuity

Periods	5%	6%	7%	8%	9%	10%	12%	14%
1	0.952	0.943	0.935	0.926	0.917	0.909	0.983	0.877
2	1.859	1.833	1.808	1.788	1.759	1.734	1.690	1.645
3	2.723	2.673	2.624	2.577	2.531	2.487	2.402	2.322
4	3.546	3.465	3.387	3.312	3.240	3.170	2.037	2.914
5	4.330	4.212	4.100	3.993	3.890	3.791	3.605	3.433
6	5.076	4.917	4.767	4.623	4.486	4.355	4.111	3.889
7	5.786	5.582	5.389	5.206	5.033	4.868	4.564	4.288
8	6.463	6.210	5.971	5.747	5.535	5.335	4.968	4.639
9	7.108	6.802	6.515	6.247	5.995	5.759	5.328	4.946
10	7.722	7.360	7.024	6.710	6.428	6.145	5.650	5.216

Here we can see why it is necessary to understand the definition of annuity. The annuity tables are calculated on the assumption that all payments begin in Year 1 (note that the first discount for the lump sum is for one year) and that the amount is the same for each year. (It must be so in order to achieve a correct answer since the yearly payment is multiplied by the annuity discount rate.) When payments are made irregularly or when the payments do not begin in Year 1, they are calculated as the sum of discounted lump sums. Using our earlier lump sum payments example and assuming a 5% discount rate:

$1000 in Year 1 = 1000 x .952   = $952
$1200 in Year 2 = 1200 x .907   = $1088
$1005 in Year 3 = 1005 x .864   = $868
                                           $2908

or :

$1000 in Year 1 $= 1000 \times .952 = \$ 952$
$2000 per year in Years 2–5

$$= 2000 \times .907 = \$1814$$
$$= 2000 \times .864 = \$1728$$
$$= 2000 \times .823 = \$1646$$
$$= 2000 \times .784 = \underline{\$1568}$$
$$\$6756$$

Caution: beginning users of financial information often make the mistake of trying to add all the years of annuity payments and multiply the result by the number from the annuity table or by a number from the lump sum table. Avoid this by understanding how the tables are constructed and when to use them. The PV of annuity should always use the yearly amount as the multiplicand and the PV of the annuity must always be less than the total of the non-discounted yearly payments.

Simple annuities and annuities due

Annuities differ according to when, during a pre-determined period, they are paid. Typically, annuity payments are made either at the beginning or the end of that period. Annuities paid at the end of a period are known as **simple annuities**. Annuities paid at the beginning of the period are known as **annuities due**. The timing of the payment has an effect on the discounting of the annuity. The first payment for an annuity due is not discounted since there is no lag between the first payment and the present. The difference between an ordinary annuity and an annuity due is illustrated below:

	Present/ begin period 1 $	End Period 1/ begin period 2 $	End Period 2/ begin period 3 $	End Period 3 $
Payment Simple annuity	0	1000	1000	1000
Payment Annuity due	1000	1000	1000	0

We have already seen how to calculate the present value of an ordinary annuity for this example. The present value for an annuity due would be calculated as follows:

Payment 1 (no discount)	
$1000 × 1	$1000
Payment 2 (discounted for 1 period)	
$1000 × .952	$952
Payment 3 (discounted for 2 periods)	
$1000 × .907	$907
Total present value for annuity due	$2859

Note that the same effect could be achieved by adding the lump-sum discount rates as we did earlier for the ordinary annuity. In this case, the amount is $2.859. There are special tables for calculating annuities due, but they can also be calculated using the tables for ordinary annuities. Note that the annuity due for three periods is actually discounted only for two of those periods. In the first year, the payment is multiplied by one. Therefore, to calculate an annuity due from an ordinary annuity table simply take the amount from the table from the next lower period and add one to it. For example, for an annuity due of three years, look down the ordinary annuity table until you reach period 2, then look across to find the number under the appropriate interest rate – 1.859 for 5% @ two years – and add 1, making it 2.859.

Using present value in decision-making

Managers are frequently faced with investment decisions that involve cash flows that occur over a number of years. Leases, for example, usually require payments for a number of years. Similarly, investments in service programs may yield revenues over a number of years. The problem managers face in such circumstances is which of the alternatives is cheaper. Since we already know that monies paid in the future have a lower value today, it becomes obvious that alternative investment decisions with cash-flows that extend further out than a single year must be discounted. The most common method of discounting investments is known as **net present value**, or NPV.

NPV and investment decisions

NPV is a decision technique used to select among investment alternatives based on their summed annual cash-flows. That is, discounted income flows are compared against discounted cash outflows.

WORKED EXAMPLE: NET PRESENT VALUE

Assume that Princes Library is considering two alternatives for acquiring their new online public access catalog (OPAC). The alternatives are to buy the system outright or to lease it. The costs associated with each alternative are as follows:

Alternative 1		Alternative 2
(purchase)		(lease) Lease cost (including all upkeep and
Equipment cost	$14,000	maintenance) $4500/year for four years
Yearly maintenance	$1,100	
Salvage value	$2,100	
(end Year 4)		

Assume that payments are made at the end of the period (i.e. as an ordinary annuity) in both cases.

A simple addition of costs makes Alternative 1 look cheaper; a more detailed analysis presents a different picture.

	Alternative 1 $	Alternative 2 $
Initial cost	14,000	0
Yearly fees	4,400	18,000
(4 × yearly fee)	_____	_____
Cost	18,400	18,000
Less salvage	(2,100)	0
Net cost	16,300	18,000

Now assume a 5% cost of capital

Initial cost	14,000	0
Discounted yearly fees		
(1100 × 3.546)	3,900	
Discounted lease yearly fees		
(4500 × 3.546)	_____	15,957
Cost	17,900	15,957
Less Discounted salvage value lump sum		
(2100 × .823)	(1,728)	_____
Net cost	16,172	15,957

As we can see, assessing the costs based on their present values now reveals the two alternatives to be much closer in cost.

The previous example looked at discounted costs for the most part. Let us examine a second investment decision that involves revenue as well:

WORKED EXAMPLE: DISCOUNTED COSTS PLUS REVENUE

Princes Library has the option of obtaining one of two different copy machines. Both machines can be used to generate revenue by charging fees to the public for making copies. The costs and revenues associated with each option are:

Option 1 (a new collating copier)

	$
Cost	4990
Yearly revenues (Years 1–3)	1000
Yearly revenues (Years 4–5)	1600
Salvage value in 5 years	1800

Option 2 – A different copier

	$
Cost	4800
Yearly revenues (Years 1–5)	1500
Salvage value (Year 5)	80

Assume the discount rate (cost of capital) is 5% and that all amounts are rounded to the nearest whole dollar. Only one example is worked for reasons of space. The second option's NPV is calculated in exactly the same manner.

	Cost $	Discounted cost $
Purchase price	4990	4990
Revenue (Years 1–3) 1000 × 2.723 (3 years at 5%)	(3000)	(2723)
Revenue Year 4 (lump sum, 5% due in 4 years) (1600 × .823)	(1600)	(1317)
Revenue Year 5 (lump sum, 5% due in 5 years) (1600 × .784)	(1600)	(1254)
Salvage (lump sum, 5% due in 5 years) (1800 × .784)	(1800)	(1411)
Total cost or (savings)	(3010)	(1715)

Revenues are calculated from the relevant annuity table. They are subtracted from the costs. Both options actually recover their costs and generate a 'profit' over their lives. This doesn't happen often, but it can and it's a desirable state of affairs.

Determining the discount rate

One of the problems frequently associated with present value calculations is setting the right discount rate. Profit-making enterprises usually find this easier since they frequently have experience calculating their cost of capital. Determining a discount rate is more problematic in not-for-profits (public sector/voluntary institutions) which do not have a benchmark profit margin on which to base returns on capital calculations.

Earlier in this chapter we discussed lending rates as a starting point for determining a discount rate. Lending rates provide a reasonable basis which can be adjusted up or down according to the nature of the investment. However, the determination of an appropriate rate is more complex than simply examining rates from banks. Project riskiness, opportunity costs of investment in one alternative over another and the degree to which the investment furthers the organizational goals are all factors which should be taken into account in setting a rate.

Rates are more useful and accurate if they are based on an empirically grounded estimate. There is no reason why you should not scan the environment and determine some baseline amount that reflects the cost of capital and adjust this according to the nature of the investment. However, an examination of the PV equation shows that the most sensitive part is usually the principal, since this is usually the largest number. In practice, this means that obtaining accurate cost estimates makes a more significant impact than 1 or 2 percentage points in the discount rate. How sensitive a given project is to changes in discount rates is discussed in the following section.

Discount rates, risk and sensitivity analysis

How much difference does it make if the discount rate is 7% instead of 8%? This question, and questions like it, are common to most decisions that involve present value calculations. Rather than discuss the issue in abstract terms, let us look at an example.

WORKED EXAMPLE: DIFFERENTIAL DISCOUNT RATES

A library has the option of leasing or buying a copier. Both alternatives have an estimated life of four years. The following costs are associated with the alternatives:

Buy	$
Purchase price	3000
Yearly maintenance	600
(paid at the end of each year.)	
Lease	
Yearly lease payments	1400

Assume the lease payments are made at the end of the year and that they include all of the maintenance costs for the copier. Comparative costs can therefore be calculated as follows.

	NPV @ 7%	8%	9%
	$	$	$
Buy			
Purchase price (not discounted)	3000	3000	3000
Yearly maintenance	2032	1987	1944
@ $600/year (assume payments			
fall due at the end of the year)	____	____	____
Total NPV	5032	4987	4944
Lease			
Yearly lease payments:	4742	4637	4536
(assume payments fall due			
at the end of the year)			

Note that there is very little difference between the three interest rates and that for the relatively short period of four years, the lease decision remains the cheaper alternative.

Imagine instead that you had been incorrect in your cost assessments and that instead of $3000, the copier actually costs $3300 and that, in your rush to make a decision, you overlooked the fact that you have to pay an additional $200 for licensing fees. The increases are not very large, but notice their effect on the NPVs of the alternatives:

	NPV @ 7% $	8% $	9% $
Buy			
Purchase price (not discounted)	3300	3300	3300
Yearly maintenance and licensing fees @ $800 (assume payments fall due at the end of the year)	2710	2650	2592
Total NPV	6010	5950	5892
Lease			
Yearly lease payments (assume payments fall due at the end of the year)	4742	4637	4536

As we can see, the changes in the principal amounts make a significantly larger impact on the costs than does one or two percentage points. This is not to say that time should not be invested in determining a discount rate, only that among the places where time can be invested in making investment decisions, as we emphasize in Chapters 2 and 3, you should devote the greatest amount of it to gathering complete and accurate cost information. Total cost, rather than the discount rate, has the greatest effect on an NPV-based decision. (Managers are strongly encouraged to become proficient in the use of a spreadsheet program to facilitate sensitivity analysis. Spreadsheets easily recalculate NPVs using different interest rates so that the net changes can quickly and easily be seen.)

Making a decision

Finances are only part of what you need to consider when you make an investment decision, and you should be wary of letting the results of an NPV analysis make the decision for you. System performance, the timing of cash flows and a variety of other non-financial factors may affect your decision to make an investment. There may also be non-rational factors such as organizational politics that are equally compelling in the decision.

You are free (or you may even be forced) to make decisions that are not optimal from a financial point of view. What is important, even in these cases, is to understand the financial implications of an investment alternative. Choosing an apparently more expensive option is not necessarily a poor decision, but it is poor decision-making to make the choice without understanding its effects on your finances. Similarly, if you decide to take a more expensive investment option for non-financial considerations it is useful to demonstrate that you were aware of the financial implications but made the choice for advantages that outweighed the larger cost. Much of what you do to invest in electronic services is persuade other levels of management to provide funding. The more competent you appear, the more likely you are to be funded.

LIFE-CYCLE COSTING REVISITED

In Chapter 2 we touched on the subject of life-cycle costing in the context of finding costs associated with an automated system. Now that we have covered the concept of present value, it is time to revisit LCC and learn how to use it to make investment decisions.

The key to using LCC is first to understand that assets that deliver the same level of service may have very different carrying costs. As we discussed earlier in the book, the purchase price of an asset may be only the tip of the iceberg. An organization's financial commitment to an asset or system grows over time and if an organization focuses only on the initial outlay of capital for purchase it may be left with an asset whose carrying costs far outweigh the price difference between it and a more expensive asset that is cheaper to operate.

WORKED EXAMPLE: CARRYING COSTS

Problem

Princes Library makes the decision to install an online reserve system. To do this requires the library to install a turnkey system that has the following components: an image scanner; a computer for storing the scanned images; access terminals; and controlling software. The library has the option of leasing or buying the equipment. The associated costs for both options are listed below. Assume a cost of capital of 5% and that the asset has an effective life of six years.

Option 1: purchase
The system can be purchased outright for a fee of $53000. Under this option, the library assumes a yearly maintenance cost of $2000/year. The asset is estimated to have a salvage value of $3000 at the end of the sixth year.

Option 2: lease
The library may also lease the same system for a yearly lease cost of $12000/year for six years. The cost includes regular maintenance with no salvage value at the end of the lease period.
    Which option should the library take?

Solution
Since the payments take place over a period greater than one year, it is necessary to discount the payments and calculate the NPV of both options in order to arrive at their total costs.

Purchase costs	$
Purchase price (not discounted)	53,000
Maintenance costs (annuity: 6 years @ 6%)	
2000 × 4.917	9,834
Total costs	62,834
Less salvage value (lump sum: 6 years @ 6%)	
3000 × .705	(2,115)
Total NPV Option 1	64,949

Lease costs	
Yearly lease (annuity: 6 years @ 6%)	59,004
12000 × 4.917	
Total NPV Option 2	59,004

Looking only at the initial purchase/lease prices the Library Director performed an NPV analysis. The lease option was clearly the cheaper over the lifetime of the asset and the director made the decision to lease. Within a year it became apparent that there was a severe drain on the library's finances. Hoping to avert a crisis, the Director reviewed all of the library investments and the following additional information came to light concerning the two options:

Option 1

1 The system needed a separate room for scanning because the scanner was so loud. The construction of a new, partitioned-off space cost $3800.
2 The machine had a history of causing eye problems because the scanner had such a bright light. New protective goggles were needed and were purchased at a cost of $190. The library insurance agent informed the Director that there was still a risk and that the library's worker's compensation premiums were to be increased by $500/year.
3 The scanner operated at a very high speed so that existing workers could keep the machine running as part of their normal duties.

Option 2

1 A new air conditioning system was needed that required an initial investment of $4000 and increased utilities costs by $1250/year.
2 The system used special storage disks that needed to be purchased from the lessor at a yearly cost of $860.
3 The library attorney was needed to review and draw up the lease contract. She charged $90/hour and averages four hours of billable time for this type of contract.
4 Freight charges for delivery of the system were $700.
5 The system required a clerical worker to deal with regular upkeep, particularly scanning. Because of the speed at which the scanner operated, keeping the system up to date required 3 hours each day of a clerk's time. Because of union regulations, however, clerks could only be hired at a minimum of half-time. The normal clerical wage (including fringe benefits) was $8/hour full-time hours in the system totalled approximately 2000 hours/year.

With this additional information, the LCCs for both options look quite different:

Purchase costs	$
Purchase price (not discounted)	53,000
Construction cost (not discounted)	3,800
Goggles (not discounted)	190
Maintenance costs (annuity: 6 years @ 6%) 2000 × 4.917	9,834
Insurance costs (annuity: 6 years @ 6%) 500 × 4.917	2,459
Total costs	69,283
Less salvage value (lump sum: 6 years @ 6%) 3000 × .705	(2,115)
Total NPV Option 1	67,168
Lease costs	
Construction costs	4,000
Freight	700
Legal Fees	360
Yearly lease (annuity: 6 years @ 6%) 12000 × 4.917	59,004
Yearly utilities 1250 x 4.917	6,146
Yearly disk purchases 860 × 4.917	4,229
Yearly additional labor ($8.00 × 1000 = $8000)	
8000 × 4.917	39,336
Total NPV Option 2	113,775

We should bear in mind that the LCCs that we calculated above are based on actual historical costs incurred after the system was installed and running and not cost estimates. In all likelihood the estimates would not have been as accurate, but there was no reason not to have investigated all of the costs associated with the system. The estimate might have been a bit less accurate than the numbers we have after the fact, but the magnitude of the differences in cost were large enough to have alerted the director to the potential financial effects of the options.

Managers are strongly urged to investigate all of the potential costs associated with any large investment before conducting an NPV analysis or making any decisions. A common error when making investment decisions is to become so involved with calculations that you forget to spend the time gathering the cost information that the calculations rely on. Your decisions will only be as good as the data that goes into them, and the omission of costs may have material, if not fatal, financial consequences.

NET PRESENT VALUE REVISITED

A net present value costing is, at best, an estimate. As we discussed earlier in the book, a poor estimate is better than none, but it is still important to keep the limitations of NPV in mind. The biggest problem with NPV as a technique is estimating the cost of capital. Depending upon the volatility of your financial environment, you may under- or over-estimate the cost of capital by a considerable margin. We have already discussed the possible effects of this and methods for estimating the effects of varying discount rates, and your reliance on NPV should be tempered by an understanding of how inaccurate your estimates may be.

You should be similarly wary of making judgments based on small differences among the NPVs of various options. How big these differences should be before they affect the decision is a matter of personal judgment and experience, but as a minimal rule of thumb, managers should treat differences of less than 10% as being comparable costs and make the decision based on other factors.

Also keep in mind that NPV is a technique for assisting decision-making. Future payments or revenues have lower values today for decision purposes. The discounted costs that you have calculated reflect only the value of future payments today. That is, this is the total cost of the investment in current dollars. For budgeting purposes you will still need to allocate the actual dollar amounts for the years in which the payments actually occur. For example, we may discount the $4500 lease payment to be made in three years as $3888 (4500 × .864) to assess its present value, but we still need to pay $4500 in Year 3.

General rules for calculating the NPV of an investment

The following is a brief, step-by-step summary of the process for making purchasing decisions.

1 Gather all relevant cost data. This is the most crucial step of the process: your calculations will only be as good as the cost estimates that go into them. Gathering cost data is the most difficult and time-consuming part of making a decision. As we have

noted, projects are frequently under-costed to the detriment of the organization's finances. Similar assets may have very different carrying costs, so it is critical to understand all of the costs associated with the asset. (Look at the life-cycle costing sections in this chapter and in Chapter 2 again to be sure you've thought of as many possible costs as you can.)

2   Categorize the cost data. Remember that all costs are relevant to your purchasing decision except sunk costs and costs which are the same across all purchase options. Investment decisions rely on future costs. Sunk costs are irrelevant since they have already been made and cannot be recovered. Similarly, costs which do not change among future alternatives have no bearing on the decision.

3   Set a discount rate. This is an art as much as a science. Scanning your environment to understand the costs of capital is a better way of estimating a rate than simply making one up. Loan rates may be a good place to start, but setting the rate is more complicated and requires an understanding of what it costs you overall to use money. Remember that a percentage point or two doesn't make as much difference in most cases as changes in the principal costs.

4   Separate the relevant costs and revenues into the following categories based on the times when they are paid and whether they are one-time or recurring costs/revenues. Table 4.3 shows which costs/revenues are discounted and how.

5   Total all of costs and all of revenues. Subtract the costs from the revenue to obtain the NPV. Some investments will yield an excess of revenues over costs, which is a desirable state of affairs from a financial standpoint. In many cases, however, there will be no revenues, only costs.

Table 4.3 Discounting costs/revenues

Payment	Discount	Method of discounting
Cost/revenue is paid/received one time immediately or within 1 year	No	N/A
Cost/revenue is paid/received one time beyond 1 year in the future	Yes	Lump sum
Costs/revenues recur regularly; payments are the same each year starting in Year 1	Yes	Annuity: use the regular payment amounts to discount
Costs/revenues recur regularly; payments are not the same each year and/or do not start in Year 1	Yes	Lump sum: discount each year's amount using the appropriate year and rate from the tables

6   Make the decision. Use the financial data to help you decide and to help 'sell' your decision as necessary. Don't let the numbers do the thinking for you, either in decision-making or persuasion. Decisions, particularly for automated systems and services, need to be made using a variety of criteria including performance, service, politics and price.

The following exercises take up where Chapter 2 left off. In Chapter 2 we examined and classified the costs. For the exercises in this chapter, we will discount the costs (where appropriate) to obtain a more accurate life-cycle cost for each investment.

EXERCISE ONE: AN INTERNET CONNECTION

Background
Assume an 8% cost of capital, an effective life of four years and that all payments are made at the end of the year.

Question
What is the NPV of the investment?

Sample answer

	40 users $	Discounted $	180 users $	Discounted	230 users $	Discounted $
1 Development and decision costs						
Attorney's fees	420		420		420	
Total discounted development costs		420		420		420
2 Purchase and installation costs						
SPARC server	15,000		4,000		6,000	
Modems	20,000		90,000		115,000	
T-1 installation	4,000		4,000		8,000	
Router	2,500		2,500		5,000	
Phone installation	1,000		1,000		2,000	
	42,500		101,500		136,000	
Total discounted purchase and installation costs		42,500		101,500		136,000
3 Yearly operating costs						
Machine space rental	300		300		600	
T-1 use	12,000		12,000		24,000	
Phone line	4,800		4,800		9,600	
	17,100		17,100		34,200	
Total discounted yearly operating costs (4 years @ 8%)						
(17100 × 3.312)		56,635		56,635		
(34200 × 3.312)						113,270
Total NPV of the investment		101,555		158,555		249,690

In this example, the costs which are discounted are those which occur in the future either as recurring costs (in which case they are discounted as annuities) or as single irregular payments (in which case they are discounted as lump sums). The costs which are discounted as annuities are payments which begin in the first period, remain the same amount for each period and continue regularly over a length of time. If all of these conditions were not met, the payments would need to be discounted as a set of individual lump sums.

EXERCISE TWO: LEASING A PHOTOCOPIER

Background
You have decided to lease a copy machine for which you have gathered the following cost information.

Estimated copies per month	2000
Estimated hours of operation per month	80
Lease cost	$200/month
Maintenance	$500/year
Electricity	$1.50/hour of operation
Toner cartridges (1 cartridge is good for 3000 copies)	$85/cartridge

Assume a useful life of four years and a discount rate of 7%.

Question
What is the NPV of the investment?

Sample answer

	Yearly	Discounted for the lifetime of the investment
	$	$
Lease cost (12 × 200)	2,400/year	
Electricity (80 × 12 × 1.50)	1,440/year	
Toner (2000 × 12/3000 × 85)	680/year	
Maintenance	500/year	
Total yearly cost	5,020/year	
NPV (5020 x 3.387)		17,003

The costs in this case have all been converted to a yearly basis, and discounted as a total. If the recurring costs have the same basis, it may be more convenient to add them first and then multiply by the discount rate from the table. In this case all of the amounts are annuities and there are no single sums to be discounted as lump sums.

EXERCISE THREE: CHOOSING AN OPAC

Background
A library manager has to choose between two stand-alone OPAC systems with the following requirements.

Option I

This option involves the purchase of a new minicomputer at a cost of $15,000. It needs a new, uninterruptable power source that will cost $2000 to install. A new room to house the computer is not needed, but the unit must be kept cooled in a 65° environment. The software changes yearly and must be upgraded at an annual cost of $3300. The system requires one-time training for two librarians at a cost of $1300. Yearly utilities are estimated at $900 for the computer and $1100 for the additional air conditioning. Maintenance is estimated to be $400 per year.

Option 2

This option involves the purchase of a larger computer at a cost of $ 26,000. Software upgrades and training are included in the purchase price. The computer has an internal battery and consequently runs adequately on a standard electrical outlet and operates at room temperature. Yearly utilities are estimated at $1000 for the computer. Maintenance is estimated at $220 per year.

Both options have an estimated useful life of five years with no salvage value. Assume a discount rate of 5%.

Question
Which option should he choose?

Sample answer

	Option I $	Discounted $	Option 2 $	Discounted $	
Equipment cost	15,000	15,000	26,000	26,000	(a)
Installation costs					
power source	2,000				
training	1,300				
Total installation	3,300	3,300	0	0	(b)
Annual operating costs					
Utilities	2,000		1,000		
Software	3,300		0		
Maintenance	400		220		
Total annual costs	5,700		1,220		
Total life cycle operating costs					
(5700 x 4.329)		24,675			
(1220 x 4.329)				5,281	(c)
Less estimated salvage value			0	0	(d)
Total life cycle NPV (a+b+c-d)		42,975		31,281	

The first thing you should notice is how much easier the tabular presentation of the numbers is to read than are the descriptive paragraphs. This is not strictly a part of making financial decisions, but much of what you do with numbers is use them to persuade and educate other decision-makers. Numbers are usually easier to read and follow when they are not treated as words and not used in a narrative style.

Again notice that regularly recurring costs are discounted as annuities. If either system had any salvage value it would need to have been discounted as a lump sum since it is a one-time future cost. The purchase prices and installation costs are not discounted since they are paid during the current year.

BIBLIOGRAPHIC NOTE

The text has presented a basic description of investment decision techniques. Readers who are interested in pursuing the subject in depth are directed to the texts listed in the references [1-4] as well as numerous other advanced finance and accounting texts. Annuity tables for different amounts and periods than those found in the text are available in numerous finance and accounting texts such as those listed below. In addition, most libraries still contain published tables of financial data including fractional percentages. Present value data are also standard features of most financial calculators and finance computer programs such as spreadsheets.

REFERENCES

1   Crowe, R., *Time and money: using time value analysis in financial planning*, Homewood, IL., Dow Jones-Irwin, 1987.
2   Kieso, D. and Weygandt, J., *Intermediate accounting*, 7th edn, New York, Wiley, 1992.
3   Kroeger, H., *Using discounted cash flow effectively*, Homewood, IL., Dow Jones-Irwin, 1984.
4   Vale, P. (ed.), *Financial management handbook*, Aldershot, Hants, Gower, 1988.

CHAPTER 5

How much do we charge?

Getting the price right is important, but it can be difficult as the following scenario suggests.

SCENARIO

Mega Library has recently decided to begin a commercial search service for local business. A small development grant has been provided by a local development agency as seed money to buy the hardware necessary to perform online searches, but it was expected that the program would become self-sustaining by charging for its services. The decision that now faces Samuel Jones (Library Director) and Jane Markham (Head of Electronic Services) is how much they should charge for the searches they were to provide.

Decision Path 1

'I haven't got any idea what to charge for a search,' said Jane. 'What do you think sounds reasonable?'

'I'm not sure either,' replied Samuel. 'What I'm really concerned about is that we don't lose money on the deal. Why don't we simply choose an amount big enough to cover any conceivable cost and see what happens?'

Jane thought this over for a moment. 'I suppose a search couldn't take more than 10 minutes of connect time. Then there's the librarian searching. I suppose $100 would cover anything that came up.'

'Let's be on the safe side and add another $50 just to be sure,' said Samuel. 'I'll advertise the service at $150.'

Six months later, they met again.

'Five months gone by and we've only had two customers,' sighed Samuel. 'I guess it's just as well we didn't invest heavily in the program. At least we didn't lose our shirt over this one.'

'Still,' said Jane, 'Princes Library seems to have a made a go of it somehow. I just spoke with the Automation Director over there and he told me his volume of search requests has increased to the point where they're having to get another terminal just to keep up. How did they do it?'

Decision Path 2

'I haven't got time to think about pricing this week,' said Jane. 'Pick any number that sounds reasonable.'

'Twenty dollars per search sound OK to you?,' asked Samuel.

'I suppose. I guess it doesn't really matter all that much. The terminal and librarian are already paid for.'

Six months later, they met again.

'That's the fifteenth request this week for a search,' moaned Jane. 'I don't know how much longer we can keep this up: I've already had to pull someone off reference.'

'I hate to say it, but I think you're right,' said Samuel. 'I don't want to close down the service. Heaven knows it's the most popular thing we do. I have no idea what it's costing us, but we're hemorrhaging cash and we can't keep it up. Who would have guessed this would be so popular?'

PRICING AND DECISION-MAKING

Libraries are increasingly faced with decisions concerning how and if services should be priced. Pricing is useful for an organization in a number of ways including recovering costs and limiting the use of scarce resources.

Our second decision path illustrates the perils of too much success in a program. If a library prices its services too low, it may lose money on a service meant to make money. Price also limits or stimulate demand for a service. Prices set too low can generate so much demand that a library's resources are overwhelmed. Public service organizations often balk at the prospect of limiting services by pricing, but the consequences of not doing so may be reducing or eliminating other services.

Some libraries have chosen to deal with the problem by setting prices so high that any imaginable costs are covered. Unfortunately, artificially high prices also have the effect of reducing demand or eliminating it altogether. A library may positively choose to discourage use of any of its services by setting prices high but, as in the case of our first decision scenario, poor pricing may keep the library from providing services that it genuinely wants and needs to provide for the community.

In the subsequent sections of this chapter we will investigate pricing and discuss various approaches to pricing, determining price levels to break-even on costs, setting price levels to encourage or discourage service provision and finally, strategies for initiating charges that will ease transition to paying for what were once free services.

For which services do we charge?

Charging for services has become a controversial topic in librarianship during the last ten years, and shows no signs of becoming less so in the future. Increasingly, libraries are encouraged to become more entrepreneurial in marketing their services, which implies charging fees for services. Critics of library fees assert that paying for services fosters the growth of information-poor users and subverts the principles of free access upon which libraries are founded.

The choice is not easy, but libraries should consider some key issues when they decide if and whom to charge, and for what. The first is that access is ultimately limited by the constraints in resources. Libraries must consider whether free access to all means reduced services to all. Charges may be the only way to afford some resources at all. A second point to consider, is how widely used are the services? If they benefit only a small portion of the library's users, it may be reasonable to expect these consumers to pay for them. Finally, libraries need to consider the ability of user groups to pay and the reasonableness of the proposal that they will do so. Groups engaged in profit-making activities generally expect, and are expected, to pay for the services that they use.

These considerations are not, of course, limited only to the provision of electronic services, but pricing issues are likely to be an integral part of any decisions involving electronic services. Since electronic services usually require costly investments in new technology and personnel, cost recovery may be the only means of offering them.

PRICE SETTING TECHNIQUES

Profit-making enterprises often discuss setting prices on a 'cost-plus' basis or according to market forces. In the latter case, customer demand and the behavior of competitors are the greatest influences on price setting. Research shows, in fact, that market forces far outweigh cost factors in many organizational pricing decisions.

If libraries are truly interested in maximizing revenue and competing in open markets, market-driven pricing may be the preferred method of price setting. Such a method requires a knowledge of markets and customers that most libraries do not have at present. Moreover, libraries and other non-profit entities are not concerned with maximizing revenue, but rather with maximizing use. In such cases, pricing based on cost assumes a greater importance.

Libraries are more likely to be concerned with recovering costs than making profits. Many libraries, in fact, might argue that they are interested in cost-minus pricing: providing subsidized services below costs. (Services may be subsidized at a lower level through grants or priced at some nominal level to keep demand within the system's capacity. See below).

Even in cases where services are offered below costs, however, accurate costing and pricing predictions are useful to predict demand and to understand the financial effects of offering a system below cost. (At what level of use can the library subsidize the service, for example?)

Which costs should be included in the price?

Organizations needing to set prices often begin by deciding between absorption and contribution costing models. These differ according to how they treat fixed costs.

Absorption costing

The structure of **absorption costing** makes the assumption that all costs, whether they are fixed or variable, need to be covered by pricing. (As we shall see, this philosophy is also implicit in contribution cost pricing.) However, full cost recovery is explicitly structured in absorption based prices. To accomplish this, a proportion of the fixed costs incurred in producing the service are included in the service cost.

WORKED EXAMPLE: ABSORPTION COSTING

Let us re-examine the standard cost for inputting a record that we set in Chapter 3 (see p.76):

	$
To input one record	
direct labor (10 minutes @ $12/hour)	2.00
Direct materials I	
forms and paper	0.20
online connect time (5 minutes @ $36/hour)	3.00
Total materials	5.20
Technical Service Department's indirect costs	
Variable (labor, supplies, etc.)	2.50
Fixed (salaries, depreciation, training, etc.)	
$50,000 divided by expected level of service = 20,000	2.50
Allocated from other Departments	
Variable	1.00
Fixed	
$22,000 ÷by expected level of service = 20,000	1.10
Standard cost to input one record	12.30

Note that a portion of the fixed costs have been allocated to the standard cost of inputting a record. If prices are set on a cost-plus basis, then a portion of the fixed costs are necessarily included in the price.

Absorption costing is often criticized because it does not accurately distinguish between fixed and variable costs. Since effective cost analysis and decision-making is usually based on the behavior of costs rather than the function of costs, managers run the risk of poor decisions if they indiscriminately use full-cost allocations. Readers are directed to Chapter 4 and the examples concerning contribution analysis for decision for a more detailed discussion.

Contribution costing

Contribution differs from absorption costing by focusing on the behavior of costs rather than their function. The contribution approach derives the basis for pricing based on the variable costs of producing a single unit of service. In contrast, absorption costing uses the total costs.

WORKED EXAMPLE: CONTRIBUTION COSTS

Using the same cost information as in the previous example for inputting a record:

	$
To input one record:	
direct labor (10 minutes @ $12/hour)	2.00
Direct Materials	
forms and paper	0.20
online connect time (5 minutes @ $36/hour)	3.00
Total materials	5.20
Technical Service Department's indirect costs	
Variable (labor, supplies, etc.)	2.50
Allocated from other Departments	
Variable	1.00
Standard cost to input one record	8.70

The variable cost of $8.70 now becomes the basis for setting the price.

Contribution-based costing is sometimes criticized for underestimating unit costs. Absorption costing, it is argued, is more accurate and produces better long-term decisions because it does not ignore the fixed costs of production. In response, it should first be noted that fixed costs can be accounted for in pricing with the contribution approach (see below for a discussion of break-even analysis). Second, the unit cost provided by absorption costing cannot be used if production volume varies.

To claim that either contribution or absorption costing produces the best pricing decisions would be misleading. Any pricing system will result in poor decisions if the manager responsible for making them lacks understanding. A more useful observation might be that accurate information concerning costs and their behavior, together with an understanding of what the organization seeks to do with pricing, usually produces useful pricing decisions.

WHAT DOES A LIBRARY WANT TO ACCOMPLISH BY SETTING PRICES?

A difficulty libraries face when they set prices centers around the issue of how much cost it may be appropriate for a library to recover. For instance, the total costs of producing CD-ROMs may be as follows.

WORKED EXAMPLE

Equipment (fixed cost)	$20,000
Set-up labor (fixed cost)	$20,000
Total fixed expenses	$40,000
Variable costs (per individual CD-ROM)	$4.50
Expected demand	5000 units

If we assume that the library wants do to no more than recover its full costs, the minimum selling price for one CD-ROM will be the variable cost plus an allocated portion of the fixed costs as follows:

Fixed cost/CD-ROM = $40,000 ÷ 5,000 units
             = $8.00

Minimum selling price/CD-ROM = $8.00 + $4.50
                  = $12.50/CD-ROM

Assuming the anticipated demand is accurate this price should recover the full cost of producing the CD-ROM.

It could be argued, however, that users should not pay for the full costs of production. Libraries usually have the explicit mission of providing information to the public rather than turning a profit. Extending this mission into financial terms, it is reasonable to argue that charges for information should be at the lowest level that makes economic sense. Since the investment costs are fixed and unvarying regardless of the number of CD-ROMs produced, there is some sense in recovering only those costs that increase with the requests. Using this argument, the costs in our example drop from $12.50 to $4.50. Considering the very high investment costs of electronic systems (and their comparatively low operating costs) the choice of price to recover full or variable costs produces a significant difference to the consumer.

The choice of a costing system may be as much a matter of ethos or at least organizational goals as of accounting. Pricing at the level of variable costs maximizes the use of the service to consumers. Pricing at full costs provides the best chance of financing future operations by recovering the cost of the assets used to provide the service. Another alternative may be to charge high prices for special services in order to subsidize more popular programs which do not have the capability of generating revenue.

PRICING AS A MEANS OF ALLOCATING SERVICES

Until this point, we have concentrated on pricing as a way of recovering costs. Pricing can also be a way of limiting use. In our scenario a low price caused the online service to become oversubscribed, which ultimately led to its closing. A higher price would have had the effect of lower demand and would have prevented overtaxing the library's resources.

If we assume that the demand for online searches is continuous and inversely related to price (i.e. higher prices produce lower demands, lower prices produce higher demand) and a fixed, maximum capacity for providing online searches, then a desirable price is one that creates a demand at or below the library's capacity.

Since the online service is limited by the assets and personnel that the library can spare to perform searches, it is reasonable to assume a fixed capacity. Exceeding this would be likely to require an increase in fixed costs. Pricing at a demand level below capacity prevents increasing fixed cost. In addition, many systems are damaged by exceeding their capacity and a lower demand reduces the likelihood that the system will be degraded.

In practice, good systems analysis and system costing estimates (see Chapter 2) allow for reasonable accuracy in estimating system costs and capacity. Demand, however, is rarely as easy to predict or as regular as the graphs of economists would lead one to believe. However, as we have stated many times throughout this text, uncertainty should not preclude making estimates. Any decision to invest in a service should be made based on some idea of the potential use of the system. Methods for deriving initial estimates might be observing similar services in other libraries, user surveys, pilot projects, etc. At a minimum a manager should be expected to have some idea of the range of demands at various prices levels and accurate cost and performance data.

WORKED EXAMPLE: PRICING TO MANAGE DEMAND

Assume the following information was available for Mega Library's online search service. Price is per search; all other costs on a yearly basis.

Table 5.1 Data for Mega Library's online search service

Price $	Range of demand	Fixed costs $	Capacity
50	400–1000	20,000	2800
30	1100–1800	20,000	2800
20	2200–3000	20,000	2800
10	3500–4500	45,000	5000

Note that at the lowest price, either demand will exceed the system's capacity or it will be necessary to increase the library's fixed costs in order to increase its ability to perform online searches. Assuming the library does not want to increase its fixed costs or exceed its ability to perform searches, the director should consider pricing at or a bit above $20.00.

The example illustrates a very simple technique for setting prices. There are many other techniques which may yield more accurate results, but which are also more complicated to perform. For many libraries, however, understanding that price affects demand, together with some knowledge of what the library's capacity is to provide the required level of services, will be sufficient to set prices that are both prudent and useful.

COST-VOLUME PROFIT RELATIONSHIPS

Break-even analysis

One of the simplest techniques used to determine the point at which a product or service repays its costs is **break-even analysis**. For activities in which we know the related fixed and variable costs, break-even analysis calculates the volume of output at which total costs equal total revenue (i.e. at which they break even – there is no profit but all costs are recovered). Break-even analysis can be used for a variety of purposes in information services and libraries including:

1   determining the number of patrons needing to use a service before it can be self-sustaining;
2   price-setting for services;
3   making investment decisions such as membership of a consortium, and
4   determining the best places for budget reductions, etc.

Subsequent sections of the chapter will examine each of these, but first let us examine how break-even analysis works.

Break-even analysis begins by separating the cost of providing a service or product into fixed and variable costs. Since many of the earlier chapters have dealt with this topic we will not devote a great deal of room to it here, except to say that accurate cost gathering and cost categorization are crucial to making break-even analysis work effectively (as they are for most financial techniques). Break-even analysis can be performed one of two ways, either of which yields equivalent results.

Method 1

Break-even point =
$$\frac{\text{Fixed cost}}{\text{Selling Price (per unit)} - \text{Variable Cost (per unit)}}$$

Method 2

Break-even point =
$$\frac{\text{Fixed cost}}{\text{Contribution margin per unit}}$$

Where the contribution margin is the difference between the selling price and the variable costs

Let us re-examine the example we used earlier for producing CD-ROMs and calculate its break-even point using both formulas.

WORKED EXAMPLE: BREAK-EVEN ANALYSIS (METHOD I)

CD-ROM costs

Equipment (fixed cost)	$20,000
Set-up labor (fixed cost)	$20,000
Total fixed expenses	$40,000

Variable costs

per individual CD-ROM	$4.50
Expected demand	5,000 units

If x is the break-even point, (BEP) using equation I is calculated as follows:

$$5000 = \frac{\$40,000}{(x-\$4.50)}$$

$5000x - 22,500 = 40,000$

$5000x \quad = 62,500$

$x \quad = \$12.50$

WORKED EXAMPLE: BREAK-EVEN ANALYSIS (METHOD II)

If Y is the contribution margin, or the difference between the selling price and the variable costs:

5000	=	$\dfrac{\$40,000}{Y}$
5000Y	=	$40,000
Y	=	$8.00

Since the $8.00 is the contribution margin, we add it to the variable cost per unit, ($4.50), to obtain a selling price of $12.50 – exactly the same answer as in the first equation above. The contribution margin approach may sometimes be more desirable if the manager is expecting a set return on the sale of each unit.

Notice that in this case we already knew the expected volume of sales and were solving for the sales price. This is often the case with new services when we have some idea of the costs and of the expected demand, but need to set a price. Managers using break-even analysis should always be careful to understand which parts of the equation are known and which they are solving for.

WORKED EXAMPLE: BREAK-EVEN ANALYSIS USING UNIT VOLUME

Let us look at a second example in which we do solve for the number of units. Mega Library has decided to undertake data entry for other libraries on a contract basis. Smaller libraries will supply Mega with their records and in return receive tapes with the input records. The prevailing rate for these services is $10/record and the Director does not believe that the library can charge more. Assuming the same costs that we calculated for obtaining a standard costs on inputting a record, what volume of input records would Mega need in order to break even on the service at a price of $10/record? (Assume for the purposes of the example that all the costs of the service will be used only for paying users.)

To input one record

	$
Variable costs per record	
Direct labor	2.00
Direct materials	3.20
Variable overhead	2.50
Allocated variable overhead	1.00
Total variable costs/record	8.70

Total fixed costs	$50,000
	$22,000
	$77,000

$$\text{BEP (number of records)} = \frac{\$77,000}{\$10 - \$8.70}$$

$$= \frac{\$77,000}{\$1.30}$$

$$\text{BEP} = 59,231 \text{ records (rounded up)}$$

Given an estimated price, the library can now decide if the market it would like to supply is large enough to pay back the costs. Calculations such as this are often useful in the planning stages of a project as an indicator of how likely a project is to repay its investment. It often happens that the volume of business necessary to repay simply does not exist. In such case it is usually wise to abandon a project that has no prospects for repayment.

Break-even and appropriations

Non-profit organizations such as libraries often receive appropriations but not revenues. That is, they receive block payments (as in the form of a grant) to offset some of the costs of service provision. When appropriations are made, it means, in effect, that fixed costs should be reduced by the amount of the appropriation:

WORKED EXAMPLE: BREAK-EVEN ANALYSIS AND APPROPRIATION

Assume the same example of inputting records as above, but with the additional information that a grant of $20,000 has been awarded to help defray the cost of inputting records as part of a larger program designed to encourage automation in small libraries. With the grant, the BEP now looks like this:

BEP (number of records)   = $$\frac{\$77,000 - \$20,000}{\$10 - \$8.70}$$

BEP   = $$\frac{\$57,000}{\$1.30}$$

BEP   =   43,846 records

With the subsidy, the market may now be large enough to allow Mega to offer a record input service.

Setting prices using break-even analysis

Managers are often faced with the decision of how much to charge in order to make a profit. As we have indicated, the decision is complex and relies to some degree on understanding market forces. Break-even analysis can help with pricing decisions by providing an index of the volume of sales that will be needed to earn a set amount of profit.

Here, using break-even analysis to set prices should begin with deciding how much money a service should earn. Numerous techniques involve internal rates of return on investments and similar benchmarks. Non-profit organizations rarely establish such internal rates, but managers usually are able to estimate the amount of money they would like to see a service return. This is then added to the fixed costs of the service to estimate whether the market is likely to supply the expected return and whether the price required is reasonable given market conditions.

WORKED EXAMPLE: BREAK-EVEN ANALYSIS AND PRICE SETTING

Let us return to the figure we used for CD-ROM production:

Equipment (fixed cost)	$20,000
Set-up labor (fixed cost)	$20,000
Total fixed costs	$40,000
variable costs	
per individual CD-ROM	$4.50
expected demand	5000 units

Assume that the Library Manager would like to see $5000 returned on the project in its first year. The calculation for the break-even (x) would be:

$$5000 = \frac{\$40,000 \text{ (fixed costs)} + \$5,000 \text{ (required return)}}{x - \$4.50}$$

$$5000 = \frac{\$45,000}{x - \$4.50}$$

$$5000x - \$22,500 = \$45,000$$

$$x = \$13.50 \text{ (selling price/CD-ROM)}$$

The director can now decide if the market will bear a price high enough to return the required amount of money. A similar analysis could be made of the number of units needed to be sold. Assume that the general market price for CD-ROMs is $14. What number of units will you need to sell?

$$\text{BEP for CD-ROMs} = \frac{\$40,000 + \$5000}{\$14 - \$4.50}$$

$$\text{BEP} = \frac{\$45,000}{\$9.50}$$

$$\text{BEP} = 4737 \text{ CD-ROMs (rounded up)}$$

In this and other cases, managers can solve for price or volume and compare the numbers generated with their knowledge of their markets to determine the likelihood of the intended service earning a required return or making back its costs.

Break-even and service level decisions

Should we accept a grant to start a new service? If we do, at what level should we offer that service? These are among the difficult decisions that managers face in relationship to grants. Most will have seen instances of grant proposals that were not large enough to cover the cost of the intended services, or programs that grew too large for the grants to cover. Accurate costing is the foundation for deciding what grants to take, but break-even analysis can be used to aid in the decision.

WORKED EXAMPLE: BREAK-EVEN ANALYSIS AND SERVICE-LEVEL DECISIONS

Assume that Mega Library faces a similar situation concerning the sale of CD-ROMs and a grant. The grant is awarded to Mega to furnish CD-ROMs, so long as the price at which they are sold does not exceed a set level (i.e. the grant is awarded to subsidize the selling of the CD-ROMs at below the cost of production). The costs are as follows.

Equipment (fixed cost)	$20,000
Set-up labor (fixed cost)	$20,000
Total fixed costs	$40,000
Variable costs	
per individual CD-ROM:	$4.50

The grant is in the amount of $100,000 with provision that Mega Library cannot charge more than $3.00/CD-ROM. At what level does the library break even?

$$\text{BEP for CD-ROMs)} = \frac{\$40,000 \text{ (fixed costs)} - \$50,000 \text{ (grant)}}{\$3.00 \text{ (maximum sales price)} - \$4.50 \text{ (variable cost)}}$$

Notice that both the fixed costs and the selling price are negative.

$$\text{BEP} = \frac{(\$10,000)}{(\$1.50)}$$

BEP =   6667 CD-ROMs (rounded up)

At the subsidized price, the library can therefore sell up to 6,667 CD-ROMs without losing money. In this case, the library offers the CD-ROMs at below cost. The library, in turn, has a $10,000 surplus (over its fixed costs) to offset the loss it incurs with the sale of each CD-ROM. The question to answer in this situation is: if each sale loses $1.50, how many will we have to make before we use up the surplus of $10,000 and begin to lose our own money? The answer in this example is 6,667 CD-ROMs.

As we know, however, lower prices often stimulate a higher demand. The library should also examine what the financial effects would be of a higher demand. Calculating the impact of higher demand does not require calculating a new break-even price. In fact, if the library has already set a price, it is usually obliged to continue offering it.

The calculation then becomes one of comparing the total cost at a given level of sales to the total revenues.

WORKED EXAMPLE: BREAK-EVEN ANALYSIS AND SHIFTS IN DEMAND

Let us suppose that the lower price increases demand. Instead of 6,667 units, the lower price prompts a demand for 7,000 CD-ROMs. What would the financial effect of this increase in demand be? Here we must use the costs and revenues at price charged.

		$
Total revenue:	(7,000 × $3.00)	21,000
Less variable expenses	(7,000 × 4.50)	31,500
Revenue less variable cost		(10,500)
Less fixed costs		(40,000)
Add grant		50,000
Total profit/(loss)		(500)

Given the cost and demand estimates that we have, the library stands to lose over $500 if it accepts the terms of the grant. In this case, the library can decide before it accepts the grant if the loss is worth it. One decision may be that the library simply cannot assume any new projects that do not make money. An alternative might be to decide that 7,000 CD-ROMs for an investment of only $500 is not a bad use of the money. In either case, the library can make the decision based on its own criteria rather than simply losing money without realizing where it goes.

Understanding the relationship between costs and revenue also suggests a number of management strategies concerning subsidized services. Just as the library loses money for every CD-ROM it supplies above 6,667, if it supplies fewer than 6,667 it generates revenue.

Imagine that only 6000 CD-ROMs are sold, the costs now look like this:

WORKED EXAMPLE: BREAK-EVEN ANALYSIS AND SENSITIVITY ANALYSIS

		$
Total revenue	(6,000 x $3.00) =	18,000
Less variable expenses	(6,000 x 4.50) = 27,000	
Revenue less variable cost	(9,000)	
Less fixed costs	(40,000)	
Add grant	50,000	
Total profit/(loss)	1,000	

At a level of 6,000 CD-ROMs, the library receives a surplus of $1000. The situation provides a range of cost-saving strategies including how intensively to promote CD-ROM sales, and which programs save the largest amounts during budget cuts. In the example, the library is better off financially to curtail their CD-ROM program and any other program with similar cost relationships.

Playing out a variety of scenarios involving various mixes of prices and estimated volume allows the library to perform sensitivity analysis with the cost-volume profit mix. As in the case of investment decisions (see Chapter 4) libraries can estimate how wrong they can be and observe the results on their finances.

Break-even analysis that does not involve setting prices

Break-even analysis can be useful in making decisions for library services that do not involve selling. Many services have different levels of pricing which may vary according to the volume of service, whether the users are members, etc.

Break-even analysis can be used in these cases to determine which payment plans are more economical, how to set prices for services and for other related cost decisions. The key here is to remember that the basic premise of break-even is to calculate at what level of service savings or sales pay back the fixed costs.

WORKED EXAMPLE: CHOICES IN JOURNAL SUPPLY

Your library has to choose between subscribing to a journal or supplying articles from it on request through the interlibrary loan system. The following cost information applies.

Journal subscription price/year $200
Cost per interlibrary loan request $12.50

At what volume of interlibrary loan requests (per year) does a sub-scription pay for itself?

$$BEP = \frac{200}{12.50}$$

= 16 requests/year are required to break even.

Therefore at 16 or more requests per year it is more economical to subscribe.

WORKED EXAMPLE: TO JOIN OR NOT TO JOIN A CATALOGUING COOPERATIVE?

You decide to do all of your cataloging on an online cooperative system; you have the option of becoming a member (by paying a yearly fee) and paying a lower price per cataloged item, or paying a higher price per item without becoming a member. The costs for the two options are as follows.

Membership fee $1500
Member cost for cataloging an item $3.20
Non-member cost per item $4.35

At what volume of cataloging does the library break even?

$$BEP = \frac{\$1500}{\text{Difference in cost per item}}$$

$$BEP = \frac{\$1500}{(\$4.35 - \$3.20)}$$

$$= \frac{\$1500}{\$1.15}$$

= 1304 items per year (rounded down)

Break-even can be used to set fees, as we illustrate in the following example.

WORKED EXAMPLE: BREAK-EVEN ANALYSIS AND SETTING FEES

A group of regional libraries has decided to start a cooperative service for interlibrary loan (ILL). Rather than have each library subscribe individually to journals, the group will compile a list of core journals and ask each library to subscribe to a portion of them. The other libraries in the consortium will request articles from the journals they don't have via interlibrary loan.

The costs associated with the venture are as follows:

Average cost of subscriptions per library	$1300/year
Average estimated number of ILL requests for a library's material (i.e. the number of times other libraries ask for copies via ILL)	115 requests/year
Cost for a library to process one request (copying, labor, postage, etc.)	$0.85/ request

How much should the cooperative charge for a request in order for a member library to break even on the subscription fees?

Subscriptions	$1300
Cost of supplying external requests (115 × $0.85)	98
Total cost	1398

$$BEP = \frac{\$1398}{\$115}$$

$$= \$12.16/\text{request (rounded up)}$$

In this case, price setting encourages each member to use the service at an equitable level. Consortia sometime foster overuse of common resources by members. Using the pricing figures from our example, each member receives the same amount in ILL fees as it spends, as long as it does not exceed the estimated level. Overuse is discouraged (or at least the supplying members are compensated for additional work) by having the charges exceed revenue for the overusing member.

MANAGING THE TRANSITION TO CHARGING FOR SERVICES

Managers often face difficulties when they are forced to charge for services. Responsibility-centered management generally requires departments to bill each other internally for services that were supplied without charge in the past. This can be very problematic for electronic or information services, since it is difficult to establish a monetary value for information.

If the information center is underused or the services it provides are unfamiliar to internal users in the organization, it is in the best interests of both the center and the organization to encourage use. Free or subsidized use is one pricing alternative that encourages increased organizational use, particularly if managers are educated in the benefits of using automated and information services. In such cases, records of service usage by relevant departments can be kept and statements issued to them at regular intervals, alerting them to the level of the resources (based, for example on standard costs) they have consumed. (Statements are distinguished in this context from charges or invoices by the fact that they are sent for informational purposes rather than with the expectation of collecting fees.) These statements will indicate patterns of usage and thus aid management in the fair allocation of future resources for information services.

Allocating the costs of the information center to various departments based on the resources available to them also encourages greater use. As we discussed in Chapter 3, allocation on the basis of potential use encourages greater use to translate the allocated cost into service output.

As information services in an organization mature, and managers become better educated in their use, it may be desirable to treat the information center as a cost center. (It makes little sense to treat it as a profit center, since it normally does not bring revenue.) In such cases, it is normally a good idea to begin the transition gradually from statements to actual charges. The change should be announced well in advance of the actual transition, so users can predict the impact on their budgets.

EXERCISE ONE: TO JOIN OR NOT TO JOIN RE-VISITED

Background
You can choose between belonging to an interlibrary loan consortium or simply using the services of the ILL consortium as an occasional paying customer. The costs of either option are as follows:

Consortium member

annual membership fee	$1000
cost per ILL request for members	$7

Non-member

cost per ILL request for non-members	$12

Question

How many yearly requests do you need to make to break even on the membership fees?

Sample answer

$$BEP = \frac{\$1000}{\text{Difference in cost}}$$

$$BEP = \frac{\$1000}{\$12 - \$7}$$

$$= \frac{\$1000}{\$5}$$

$$BEP = 200 \text{ requests}$$

At 200 requests/year the library breaks even. At more than 200 requests, it is cheaper to become a member. The key to understanding these situations is to realize that the membership fee is the fixed cost: members pay regardless of the number of requests they make. The fee, however, provides a discount for each ILL request. The task then is to determine at what level of service the discount pays back the initial fixed cost of membership.

EXERCISE TWO: DIFFERENTIAL CONNECTION TARIFFS

Background

Your local phone company offers the following options on local service:

Plan One: payment for single calls

A single fee of $.06 for each call regardless of the time.
A usage charge of $.025 for each minute the call takes after the first minute.

Plan Two: unlimited time

A single monthly fee of $43.00.
A single fee of $.02 for each call with no additional charges regardless of the duration of the call

You have kept a log book for three months and have concluded that the average time that library staff spend on a call is 7 minutes.

Question

What volume of calls do you need to make in order to break even on the unlimited usage charge?

Sample answer

The key is first to calculate the cost of an average call, in this case seven minutes. Under Plan One, the cost of an average call is calculated as follows:

	$
First minute (regardless of duration)	0.06
Usage fee	
(6 minutes @ $0.025/minute)	0.15
Average cost/call	0.21

Notice that the cost is calculated using 6 minutes since the cost is for each minute after the first minute.

$$\text{BEP (number of calls/month)} = \frac{\text{fixed cost/month}}{\text{Difference in charge}}$$

$$= \frac{\$43}{\$0.21 - \$0.02}$$

$$= \frac{\$43}{\$0.19}$$

$$= 226 \text{ calls/month (rounded down)}$$

This example is similar to the one above. The purpose is to understand at what level of service the discount pays back the fixed monthly cost. Notice that an accurate understanding of phone use is necessary to perform a useful analysis.

REFERENCES

Readers who want more detail on pricing decisions and strategies are referred to the references.[1-3]

1 Arnold, J., *Pricing and output decisions*, Accountancy Age Books, London, 1994.
2 Hoshower, L. and Verstraete, A., 'Accounting for information center costs', *Journal of accounting and EDP*, Winter, 1986, 4–9.
3 Kingsma, B., *The economics of information*, Libraries Unlimited, Englewood, Co, USA, 1996.

CHAPTER 6

Conclusion

ASSETS IN LIBRARY INFORMATION SERVICES

A 1993 US Public Library Association survey[1] indicates that the median budget for even a a small library (serving a population of 10,000–25,000) is over $229,000, 'below Wall Street standards, but large enough to be tempting', as Snyder and Hersberger observe in their introduction to a study of fraud in US libraries.[2] Libraries and information services make significant purchases of inventory, administer large payrolls, take in large sums of cash and generally control budgets as large and complex as those of many private corporations. As a result, the efficient use of assets to accomplish the goals of a service has become a key component of information services administration.

REVIEW

In the previous chapters we introduced you to various concepts and techniques (listed in full in the Glossary) which should enhance the efficient use of assets. In Chapter 1, we covered basic costing terminology, and showed you how to assess the time dimensions of resource management and how to differentiate between assets and expenses on the basis of benefits expected and benefits achieved. In the second chapter, we looked at fixed and variable costs as a starting point for discriminating among levels of service. In Chapter 3, we introduced concepts relating to cost allocation, cost centers and levels of responsibility These concepts will allow you to determine where the boundaries of accountability lie in a given organizational context. We considered the consequences of different methods of cost allocation, with particular focus on overheads, and introduced the concept of standard costing, which can serve as a measure of performance for resources at different levels in the organization.

In Chapters 4 and 5, we moved from 'simple' costing to techniques which take account of the time value of money in the context of long-term investment (using present and future value), and to approaches to price setting which build on the definitions of fixed and variable costs presented in earlier chapters. With these chapters behind you, you should be able to assess whether and at what level investments or proposed products and services become viable.

EXTENSIONS OF COST ACCOUNTING

In addition to their use as routine costing methods or costing approaches to one-off projects, the techniques which we have introduced have value as approaches to performance measurement. Cost variance analysis, for example, can indicate to what extent a proposal has been adequately assessed. Performance measurement is a subject too large to tackle here, but we refer the reader who wishes to explore this aspect of cost accounting to the text by Bryson, as a first port of call.[3] A second avenue you may wish to explore is the protection of assets. It is not enough to be able to use assets efficiently: those managers who are concerned with the efficient use of assets should also be concerned with evaluating, protecting and preserving them. To do this, internal control is necessary.

INTERNAL CONTROL

Internal control can be defined as the 'plan of organization and all of the coordinate methods and measures adopted within a business to safeguard its assets, check the accuracy and reliability of its accounting data, and encourage adherence to prescribed managerial policies.'[4]

Although it is concerned with the management of financial assets, internal control is not purely an accounting function; more generally, it is a set of guidelines for all managers. Protection of assets from loss or theft cannot occur effectively if it is left solely to the library financial manager or accountant. As we shall see, many of the elements of an internal control program are part of the daily operations of any organization. Library and information services administrators are not, of course, expected to be experts in internal control, but most of the principles of internal control are rooted in common-sense approaches to managing finances and it will become apparent that the most basic steps taken to protect the assets of a library through internal controls will yield levels of protection and control that far outweigh the cost of setting them up.

Why internal control is important in information services

Any organization is concerned to control its assets effectively, but internal control is a pressing issue in library and information services for two reasons.

Growth of assets

Assets in this area have grown to such an extent that more sophisticated management is needed to preserve them. The electronic provision of services has brought more equipment into the library and particularly where these services are distributed externally as well as internally, greatly complicated management's task. Libraries and information services are often thought of as having little that is worth stealing. This may be true by the standards of corporate crime, though, as we indicate above, but the median budget for a small library is not insubstantial. Similarly, many libraries routinely handle sometimes considerable amounts of cash generated by fines and user fees. Informal systems that may work in smaller, less complicated organizations will not be sufficient to manage assets in large, multidepartmental libraries, or in consortial environments, where access to a number of different 'asset bases' is greatly enhanced. In many cases, the internal control procedures of libraries have not kept pace with the growth in their assets, leaving the library with inadequate protection against loss.

Shrinking budgets

Shrinking budgets are forcing libraries and information services to exercise tighter control over their assets. Internal control does more than deter financial misconduct: it is also a means of maintaining better control of assets. Faced with a future of smaller budgets and the challenge of maintaining reasonable levels of service with fewer resources, or by means of jointly shared resources, libraries must be able to control and eliminate waste and get the most out of the assets they have.

Together, these changes to the internal procedures and administration of library and information services, and to the environments in which they operate, are of such magnitude that good internal control has become central to successful operations and in some cases, to survival.

Elements of internal control

Specific internal control programs may vary, but all operate on the same principles. These principles are often referred to as 'elements' (or a checklist) of internal control, and can be applied equally to electronic as to non-electronic library and information services. These elements can be used to evaluate any organization's internal control procedures (Horngren).[4] The checklist discussed in this article was originally formulated by Ahrens and Loebbecke,[5] and subsequently modified by Horngren, and is standard in the accounting field. The elements in the list include:

reliable personnel;
physical safeguarding of assets;
separation of duties;
adequate documentation;
independent checks; and
proper procedures and authorizations.

As is the case with performance measurement, internal control is a topic which merits coverage in its own right. Readers who wish to pursue it are referred to the texts mentioned above and to that by and Snyder and Hersberger.

THE COST OF CONTROL

It is a truism of internal control that organizations always underwrite the cost of losing assets. All that remains is the question of how they want to do it. Basic accounting systems are integral to operating any organization effectively whether it is public or private. But beyond basic organizational record keeping, managers need to analyze the 'costs of keeping the cost'. Does the cost of maintaining the internal controls that provide better control and reduce the risk of financial misconduct outweigh the potential losses that could result by not having them?

Unfortunately, it is often difficult to determine the benefits of additional scrutiny. Comparing the benefits of an internal control system with a loss that has already occurred is a compelling but not very efficient method. Instead, library managers need to assess the potential for loss in a given task or position and compare this with the cost of providing additional internal control. In some cases, it may be more cost effective simply to allow the loss to occur. An important consideration, however, is that most losses are the result of casual temptation.

No control system will be foolproof, of course, and the aim of internal control is not to create an operationally perfect system or one which is impervious to all crime. Errors will always occur while ingenious criminals will always find a way round even the best system. Rather, the task of library and information services managers should be to create a system of internal controls that provides a cost-effective means of minimizing loss and reducing temptation.

There are other internal control areas where the manager of a library or information service must be vigilant: such breaches of privacy and breaches of intellectual property (including copyright) law, for example. As the focus of this book is cost and management accounting, we have not attempted to cover these topics though they have been amply discussed elsewhere in, for example, Stallings,[6] and Gurnsey.[7]

RECOMMENDED PRACTICE

A number of texts in the UK cover financial misconduct. The UK's Chartered Institute of Public Finance and Accountancy has published manuals such as CIPFA, 1995,[8] which spell out in differing levels of detail both mandatory and voluntary practices, and the role of various watchdog bodies such as the Consultative Committee of Accountancy Bodies (CCAB), the Audit Commission, and the Auditing Standards Board (ASB), all of which issue statements of standard accounting practice (SSAPs). The Chartered Institute of Public Finance and Accountancy has also issued a number of texts which specifically address internal audit such as Anderson[9] and CIPFA Duties.[10] In a review of public service accounting standards (CIPFA, 1995), CIPFA analysts review internal audit practice in a number of national jurisdictions, and recommend the formation of a body based on the Federal Accounting Standards Advisory Body in the United States.

Liabilities and legal responsibilities are covered in the CIPFA literature. In the case of local authority library and information services, the design of financial control systems is unlikely to be the responsibility of a departmental manager, who will in most cases simply operate in accordance with standard procedures adopted by the relevant authority (CIPFA/ LASAAC),[11] and administered by an internal auditor, who is 'external' to any given department in that authority. In the case of fraud, however, CIPFA (CIPFA Investigation),[12] make it very clear that vigilance is required of every manager. The authors of that particular report conclude that the first line of defence for an organization against fraudulent acts 'must be the establishment and maintenance of efficient financial management'. We would go further: 'an understanding of cost and pricing practices and of the information gathering that lies behind those practices can improve not only decision-making in your library or information service, but also the integrity of the entire operation.'

REFERENCES

1 Public Library Association, *Statistical report 1993*: special section: 'Public library finance survey', Chicago: Public Library Association, 1993.
2 Snyder, H., and Hersberger, J., 'Public libraries and embezzlement: an examination of internal control and financial misconduct', *Library quarterly*, **67** (January, 1997), pp 1–23.

3 Bryson, J., 'Budgeting and economic analysis'. In *Effective library and information centre management*, London, Gower, 1990, 345–73.

4 Ahrens, A., and Loebbecke, J., *Auditing: an integrated approach*, 2nd edn, Englewood Cliffs, NJ, Prentice Hall, 1980.

5 Horngren, C., *Cost accounting: a managerial approach*, Englewood Cliffs, NJ, Prentice Hall, 1982.

6 Gurnsey, J., *Copyright theft*, London, Aslib/Gower, 1995.

7 Stallings, W., *Protect your privacy: the PGP user's guide*, Englewood Cliffs, NJ, Prentice Hall, 1996.

8 CIPFA, *Setting accounting standards for public services: the time for change*, London, CIPFA, 1995.

9 Anderson, M., *Internal audit made simple*, London, CIPFA, 1989.

10 CIPFA; Féderation des experts comptables européens, *The duties and responsibilities of internal audit: ideas from the United Kingdom*, London, CIPFA, 1994.

11 CIPFA/LASAAC, *Code of practice on local authority accounting in Great Britain*, London, CIPFA, 1995.

12 CIPFA, *The investigation of fraud in the public sector*, 2nd edn (fully revised), London, CIPFA, 1994.

Glossary of terms used in the text

Absorption costing

The structure of absorption costing makes the assumption that all costs, whether they are fixed or variable, need to be covered by pricing. Full cost recovery is explicitly structured in absorption-based prices. To accomplish this, a proportion of the **fixed costs** incurred in producing the goods or the services is included in the service cost. Absorption costing is held to produce better long-term decisions because it does not ignore the fixed costs of production.

Activity-based costing

Activity-based costing attempts to assign overhead costs in relation to the activities that cause them, rather than on a more arbitrary basis. Traditionally, overhead has been treated as having little or no causal relationship with levels of service, but ABC operates on the premise that many of the costs usually treated as overhead are, in fact, variable costs. A closer examination of overhead costs can uncover cause and effect relationships linking activities with overhead costs, and so help identify the activity that causes or drives that cost.

Annuities

It is usual for organizations to receive income as a steady stream of payments paid at regular intervals. In finance, these payments are known as annuities. In order for a stream of payments to be an annuity, it must meet the following conditions: the payment must begin in the first period of the payback time and the amount of the payment must be the same in each period. Annuities can also be calculated by adding together the present values of individual **lump sums.**

Annuities due

Annuities paid at the beginning of the period are known as annuities due. The timing of the payment has an effect on the discounting of the annuity. The first payment for an annuity due is not discounted since there is no time lag between the first payment and the present time.

Appropriation

Non-profit organizations such as libraries often have appropriations but not **revenues**, that is, they receive block payments (in the form of a grant) to offset some of the costs of providing a service. When appropriations are awarded, it means in effect that **fixed costs** are reduced by the amount of the appropriation

Asset

An asset is defined as a resource from which the organization expects to get benefit in the future. The concept of future benefit is particularly important because it is this that distinguishes assets from **expenses**. The timing of the receipt of a benefit is one of the features that distinguishes assets from expenses.

Bailout payback analysis

The simple method of **payback analysis** answers the question: 'What is the payback period for my project if it goes as well as expected?' Many projects carry varying degrees of risk when it also becomes important to answer the question: 'Which investment offers the best protection if something should go wrong and we're forced to abandon the project?' The analysis of payback that concerns risk is usually known as the 'bailout payback period'. In such cases, the salvage value of the investment needs to be taken into account as well as the payback.

Break-even analysis

One of the simplest techniques used to determine the point at which a product or service repays its costs is break-even analysis. For activities in which we know the related **fixed** and **variable** costs, break-even analysis calculates the volume of output at which total **costs** equal total **revenue** (i.e. the point at which they break even – no profit but all costs are recovered). Break-even analysis begins by separating the costs of providing a service or product into fixed and variable costs.

Cash-flow

Cash-flow is the movement of cash resources in or out of the organization as when I write a check for $1000 for the computer (cash resources flow out) or when a customer gives me $500 for online searches (cash resources flow in). Cash-flow is concerned with the availability of funds in an organization; this is important from the managerial standpoint because the ability to make payments and receipts is a fundamental part of running an organization. Remember that cash-flow is not synonymous with **expense** or **revenue**.

Contribution costing

Contribution costing differs from absorption costing in that it focuses on the behavior of costs rather than on their function. The contribution approach assumes that the basis for setting prices is the **variable costs** of producing a single unit of a product or service. In contrast, absorption costing uses the total costs as its basis.

Contribution-based costing is sometimes criticized for under-estimating unit costs, but it should be noted that **fixed costs** can be accounted for in pricing while using the contribution approach.

Cost accounting

Cost accounting is a form of financial management which, assuming it conforms to established practice, remains constant across different activities, programs and institutions. It is used to determine whether resources have been used effectively. Simply, it is the process of classifying the resources associated with an activity, then attributing a monetary value to them and collating the monetary cost to show the cost of the activity. In libraries, the practice falls into two categories: routine costing which is used to provide regular financial and management information, and special exercise costing, which deals with specific projects and activities.

Cost allocation

The allocation of the **costs** associated with a particular activity or range of activities helps the organization to be aware of and manage the inevitable increases or decreases in such costs. The criterion of cause and effect should be the starting point for allocation of costs as either **fixed costs** or **indirect costs**. However, since completely accurate cost usage information is often costly, if not impossible, to obtain an alternative approach that approximates usage by various subunits of an organization is necessary. As a minimum, a flat fee, regardless of the level of usage expected by the department incurring the costs, may be desirable if only to let managers know that they are incurring them.

Cost centers

Cost centers are areas of responsibility or activity in which a manager is accountable for the cost incurred by those areas. A reference department would be an example of a cost center if its director has responsibility for controlling the costs of providing a reference service. A cost center may contain many or few **cost objectives**. It is important to remember that simply knowing what the costs for an activity are does not mean that a manager is able to control them: no control, no cost center.

Cost objectives

Costs need to be 'about' something. This 'something' is the cost objective and may be running a reference desk, an online search performed for a customer, setting up a LAN, or any other activity such as restructuring, resource-sharing initiatives, mergers and out-sourcing. Cost objectives may be activities over which a manager has control, but managerial control is not a necessary characteristic of a cost objective.

Cost pools

Costs can be pooled (i.e. grouped together or aggregated) in a variety of ways including whether they are **fixed** or **variable** and/or according to their degree of homogeneity, that is, how similar are they in their causal relationship to the cost objective. Costs most commonly pooled are those relating to departments and to products.

Cost-minus pricing

Libraries are more likely to be concerned with recovering costs and breaking even than making profits. Thus, many libraries will argue that they are more interested in cost-minus than in cost-plus pricing – in providing subsidized services at or below cost. Services may be subsidized at a lower level through appropriations or grants or priced at a level designed to keep demand within the system's capacity.

Costs

Costs are resources that have been exchanged (in terms of their cash value) with cash or other resources of equal value with the expectation that they will produce future value. As the benefits of costs are realized, the costs are said to 'expire'. Expired costs are defined as **expenses**.

Unexpired costs (costs which are still expected to produce future benefits) are defined as **assets**.

Depreciation

An **asset** is usually assumed to be worth less over time and it is therefore said to 'depreciate'. Depreciation allows for this lessening in value. One way to approach this is to divide the cost of the asset by its effective life in years. This assumes that for each of n life years of the asset, $\$n$ of resources leaves the organization. This is called straight-line depreciation. An alternative method assumes that an asset depreciates at $\$n$ per year but that this does not represent a loss of operating funds. Remember that depreciation does not affect **cash-flow** in subsequent years – in other words, cash and value are not the same.

Direct cost allocation

Direct allocation is the easiest method of **cost allocation** to implement, and as a result is widely adopted in many organizations. It ignores services rendered by one department to another and allocates each service department's costs entirely to the service producing departments.

Direct costs

Direct costs are those costs that can be traced to a particular **cost objective**.

Discount rate

In the case of the **present value** method of valuing funds, the interest rate is referred to as the discount rate or cost of capital. This is the price that the organization pays to use money. Borrowing rates are useful as the starting point for determining the discount rate, but the concept involves more than loans.

Efficiency variance

Efficiency variances are calculated by taking the difference or **variance** between the actual quantity of an input and the budgeted quantity of an input needed to achieve a predetermined actual level of output, and then multiplying it by a budgeted unit price.

Expenses

An expense is generally defined as an outflow of resource that is attached to a particular period in time – usually the current operating year. Expenses are resources for which there is no **future value** – only a current value. An example is $100 for an electricity bill for the month of May: you have consumed electricity and have paid for it and there is no expectation of future value.

Financial accounting

Financial accounting is the generic term for the public reporting and disclosing of the financial records of an organization according to a range of professional and legal standards. These standards specify how and for what expenses may be recognized, where on an income and expenditure statement they are lodged, and so on. Financial accounting is used for preparing financial reports for external consumption to a universally acceptable standard.

Fixed costs

Costs are categorized as fixed or **variable** according to the ways in which they change in relationship to changes in levels of activity. Activities may be measured in hours of operation, individuals served, questions answered, searches performed or in ways the organization desires. The cost of an activity is fixed if it remains unchanged despite fluctuations in activity levels.

Flexible budget variance analysis

A flexible budget can be adjusted for changes in the volume of output. Note that the unit prices for costs remain constant in this kind of budget so that the **variance analysis** focuses on the effects of changes in volume at the aggregate level.

Future value

The value of money does not remain constant over time as the compound interest earned in a savings account shows. Money that is placed on deposit today will have a higher value in the future as a result of the interest it accrues. The money accrues interest not only on the original amount deposited (known in finance as the 'principal') but also on the accrued interest that is redeposited – the "compounding' portion of compound interest. In finance, this higher value is referred to as future value (FV) and it can be computed using the following formula:

Future value = Principal × (1+ interest rate) period on deposit

Ideal cost standards

There is some disagreement as to whether the standards used for **standard costing** should be ideal or practical. Ideal standards are usually defined as those that can be met only under optimum conditions. Proponents of ideal standards suggest that the "pull' aspects of very high standards are motivational. However, standards that can rarely or never be met may cease to be effective either as a motivation or as a standard.

Indirect costs

Organizations also have indirect costs, sometimes known as overhead which are common to a variety of **cost objectives** and cannot be attributed easily and directly to any single one. Administrative costs are a common example of indirect costs

Liabilities

Liabilities are defined as anything for which a legal claim may be made against the **assets** of an organization. In many cases you may purchase things not for cash, but on credit. Imagine, that a $1200 computer is purchased with a credit loan rather than with cash. At the time the computer comes into the building, there is no cash flow, but the computer seller has a legal claim against your assets for $1200. If you didn't pay, they could take you to a debt collection agency to recover the money. Assume you are paying for the computer at the rate of $100 a month with no interest payments; every month $100 of cash flows out of the organization which reduces the liability, but you do not gain additional value: all you are doing is reducing your obligations.

Life-cycle costing

Life cycle costing (LCC) is a decision-making technique that attempts to take into account all of an asset's **costs** during the lifetime of the **asset** associated with those costs. There is no set formula for incorporating all of an asset's costs in an estimate, so it may be more useful to think of LCC as framework for examining the cost of assets that highlights areas where costs may be incurred.

Lump sum
A lump sum is a single payment paid at one time and in the future.

Managerial (or management) accounting
Managerial accounting is that activity that supplies financial information to managers in order that they may make decisions about the organization in which they work. The reports produced are for internal consumption only, and the way in which they are produced may vary across organizations. **Cost accounting** has to a large extent been subsumed under managerial accounting.

Market-driven pricing
Market-driven pricing of goods or services offered for sale requires a knowledge of markets and customers and is most suited to profit-making organizations who are concerned with maximizing **revenue.**

Mixed costs
Mixed costs are those costs that exhibit properties of **fixed costs** at some levels of activity and properties of **variable costs** at other levels. Telephone charges are an example of this type of mixed costs. Customers typically pay a fixed amount (say $50/month) simply to have a telephone connection regardless of the volume of calls made. Additional amounts based on the number of minutes of calling time (say $0.50/minute) used are also payable.

Net present value
NPV is a decision-making technique used to select one investment option from a number of alternatives on the basis of their summed annual **cash flows.** That is, discounted income flows are compared against discounted cash outflows.

Payback analysis
Payback analysis is a measure of the time that it takes to repay the initial investment in an **asset** or program or project. Given an initial outlay of capital and a projected set of uniform **cash-flows,** payback provides an estimate of when an investment will repay its initial costs. The formula for calculating the payback period is as follows:

$$\text{Payback period} = \frac{\text{Incremental capital investment}}{\text{Yearly cash inflow from investment}}$$

Practical cost standards

Practical cost standards, unlike **ideal cost standards**, are defined as "tight but reasonable'. That is, the standard is one that may reasonably be achieved by a highly efficient and motivated worker. **Variances** from practical standards (i.e. where more or less expense is incurred for a given unit) usually provide better information to managers since they show a difference in cost from what a normal, efficient worker would produce.

Present value

In finance terms, the lower value that funds paid in the future have today is known as present value. The formula used to calculate **future value** is the reciprocal of that used for present value:

$$\text{Present value} = \frac{\text{Principal}}{(1 + \text{interest rate}) \text{ periods before payment}}$$

Price setting

Price setting (or 'fixing') can be done in a number of ways. Profit-making enterprises usually set prices either on a 'cost-plus' basis or according to market forces. In the latter case, customer demand and the behavior of competitors are the greatest influence on the price set. Research shows that market forces are far more important in organizational pricing decisions than are cost factors. There are many techniques for price setting which yield accurate results, but some are complex. For many libraries and information services it will probably be sufficient to understand how price affects demand and to have some knowledge of the library's capacity to provide any given product or service. This will allow you the manager to set prices that are both prudent and useful. Managers will usually estimate how much they would like to see returned in revenue from sales of a product or service given its capacity to offer them. This is then added to the **fixed costs** of the product or service to determine whether a sufficient market exists to supply the expected return or if the price needed is reasonable given market conditions.

Price variance

Detailed **variances** can be calculated for any variable inputs – direct labor, direct materials and variable overhead – providing that standard costs have been derived for these inputs. Price variances are calculated by taking the difference between the actual and budgeted costs of an input, then multiplying the result by the number of output units produced.

Revenue

Revenue is an in-flow of resources into an organization. It is straightforward in most not-for-profits in that in these organizations, managers are usually supplied with operating funds to operate by an external source. There is one important feature of revenue in a not-for profit organization, in terms of cash receipt – when you receive funds for providing a specific service that has not yet been provided, whoever provides those funds has a legitimate claim against the monies they have given you. You as a manager cannot therefore recognize it as revenue until you have spent the money in ways that the organizational commitment says you have to.

Revenue centers

Where a manager has the ability to control the inflow of funds through marketing and pricing decisions his or her area of responsibility will be described as a revenue center.

Simple annuity

Annuities differ according to when, during a given time period, they are paid. Typically, annuity payments are made either at the beginning or the end of that period. Annuities paid at the end of a period are known as simple annuities.

Standard costs

Standard costs may be defined as the criteria or benchmarks against which performance can be measured. Standard costs are predetermined levels of what it should cost to produce a unit of a given product or service. The use of standard costs provides a number of benefits to managers including easier, cheaper costing and an increased awareness of costs among all employees who may therefore become more cost-conscious and hence more economical in their work. They may be **ideal** or **practical**.

Static budget variance analysis

We can think of **variance analysis** occurring at various levels of detail. The most basic variance analysis would be a comparison of a static budget with the actual costs of producing units of a service or product at a predetermined level. Comparison against static budgets is the easiest variance analysis to perform, but it also provides the least useful information to managers since static budgets are limited to a single level of production of goods or a service that may not be reflected by the actual amounts.

Step-down costing

Step-down costing requires each department to allocate its **costs** to all remaining departments in the organization regardless of whether they produce a service or product. Each of those departments then allocates its total costs in turn, until all of the organizational costs are passed on to the final products or services. As each department's costs are allocated, the total costs of the department are reduced to zero and the department ceases to be part of the **cost allocation** process.

Sunk costs

Sunk costs are costs for which an outlay has already been made and which cannot be affected by any current decisions. An example of a sunk cost might be the non-refundable purchase of a computer for $5000. Sunk costs, and indeed historical costs of any sort, are no basis for making future decisions although they may be the best (or indeed the only) predictor of future costs.

Variable costs

Costs are categorized as **fixed** or variable according to the ways in which they change in relation to changes in levels of activities. Activities may be measured in hours of operation, individuals served, questions answered, searches performed or any other index of activity. A cost is variable if it changes in direct proportion to fluctuations in relevant activity levels.

Variance analysis

Managers typically make decisions concerning inputs to the production of services that involve two variables: the price of inputs and the quantity of inputs. The use of **standard costs** allows managers to assess the performance of a department by comparing its budgeted costs and the quantities of inputs used to provide a particular level of output with the actual costs of providing that output and then analyzing the difference (the variance).

Index